SEATTLE
PICNICS

Favorite Sites,
Seasonal Menus,
and
100 Recipes

BY BARBARA HOLZ SULLIVAN

Alaska Northwest Books™
Anchorage • Seattle

To Jerry— I couldn't ask for a better picnic companion.

And to Oscar and Carol, my ideal picnicgoers. Curious, creative, inexhaustible, and respectful, they first explore the history, flora, and fauna of a picnic destination at the library to better appreciate its distinct character once they arrive. They create uncommon dishes to share; they set out in any kind of weather; and they observe, touch, and might even taste their surroundings, but never alter it for those who follow.

———

Library of Congress Cataloging-in-Publication Data
Sullivan, Barbara Holz, 1941–
    Seattle picnics : favorite sites, seasonal menus, and 100 recipes /
by Barbara Holz Sullivan.
      p. cm.
    Includes index.
    ISBN 0-88240-408-3
    1. Picnicking. 2. Picnic grounds—Washington (State)—Seattle—
Guide-books. 3. Outdoor cookery—Washington (State)—Seattle.
4. Seattle (Wash.)—Description and travel—1981— —Guide-books.
I. Title.
TX823.S95   1991
641.5'78—dc20   91-8398
                                  CIP

Book design by Graphiti Associates, Inc.
Cover illustration by Laura M. Pollack

Alaska Northwest Books™
A division of GTE Discovery Publications, Inc.
22026 20th Avenue S.E.
Bothell, WA 98021

Printed in U.S.A. on acid-free paper

CONTENTS

PREFACE

I grew up in a midwestern German community where every conversation and piece of correspondence was laced with descriptions of food. Recipes were exchanged, menus analyzed, and new taste discoveries talked about. The very essence of nurturing lay in the daily meal preparation, weekly baking, and the seasonal gardening, gathering, and canning that occurred in everyone's household. A table did not hold a proper meal unless it included meat, potatoes, bread, vegetables, soup, and dessert—all homemade and laden with sauces, gravies, and frostings.

Picnics were anticipated with more pleasure than almost any other food occasion. It took my mother two days to prepare for each excursion, whether the outing was destined for one of the many parks on the bluffs overlooking the Mississippi River or for the overgrown play yard of a one-room country schoolhouse.

My family held an outdoor feast for each season: we gathered watercress in spring, picked wild black raspberries in the summer, and each fall, foraged for butternuts, hickory nuts, and black walnuts. The overflow was transported home to preserve for later enjoyment.

P r e f a c e

I have carried my Midwestern love affair with food and picnics to the Pacific Northwest where there are unlimited opportunities to be creative, both in selecting a picnic site and in planning a menu. For me, matching the Northwest's wide selection of beautiful picnic sites with its abundance of fresh and tasty food is a logical and natural continuation of those first picnics with my family.

Finally, it is my hope that you will use the food and site suggestions in *Seattle Picnics* as an impetus to explore the area's rich history and cultural diversity, as well as its beautiful picnic spots.

PICNIC MENUS

Picnics should be fun and sponta-
neous. This book encourages you to make your outings as carefree
as possible by selecting from its many themes, menus, recipes (only
the recipes with asterisks in the menu are included), sites, and, if
you're so inclined, local markets that provide picnic fare (see Sources
for Picnic Foods at the back of the book) ready to go—all suited to
various seasons and occasions.

You'll find that a theme helps
unify picnic planning, from selecting a location to choosing a menu
to picking napkin colors. The suggestions that follow offer a wide
range of choices: ethnic and seasonal, classic and cute. You can build
on these ideas to create your own special picnics—instead of a
Teddy Bear's Picnic, why not a Mad Hatter's Tea?

For a time, I became obsessed with
creating original themes. I even devised one called "A Mockery":
a mock picnic in a mocked-up park. The menu: mock turtle soup,
mock chicken legs (made from artfully skewered pork chunks rolled
in cornflake crumbs), mock apple pie, mock orange blossom tea.
Mood: false gaiety. Decorations: a mock moon in a false dawn, false
faces worn by false-hearted guests spouting falsehoods, afraid to

make a false step. Clearly I was becoming crazed, so I forced myself to stop at thirty-two picnics.

The menus in this book are merely suggestions. Most readers will mix and match the courses; others will head for the ready-made dishes at Larry's Markets or QFC and never try the recipes. That's fine, because nearly every recipe has its counterpart at one of our region's excellent markets. I enjoy fixing dishes from scratch, giving each my signature. And when I make something myself, I'm assured that my creations contain no hidden preservatives or tainted ingredients.

Experiment with substitutions and your own inventions. A picnic need not be elaborate: a colorful medley of fresh seasonal salad ingredients, a loaf of country French bread, and a bottle of wine are really all you need. Other simple yet elegant choices include water crackers topped with slivers of smoked salmon and lightly sprinkled with lemon juice and capers; caviar on thin, crisp toast; slices of Cougar Gold on bread; chilled fruit such as tiny champagne grapes and Bing cherries; or a selection of sushi or sashimi.

During your lunch hour or before turning out your bedside lamp at night, take time to read through the menus and recipes in order to choose and plan. A few dishes need advance preparation; several others taste better when prepared a day or two ahead. Still others can be frozen until you (and the weather) are ready for a spontaneous outing.

The menus contain suggestions for beverages, generally for one alcoholic and one nonalcoholic drink. Although public parks and beaches prohibit alcohol, I have suggested a few picnic spots where it can be consumed in moderation.

Seattle Picnics is not meant to limit you, rather to serve as a springboard for your own ideas. Picnics can be robust and hearty or minimalist and spare—prairie-school or Gothic, take your pick. I've tried to tempt you with a variety of tastes.

And remember, recipes are living folklore: food-story transferred from great-grandmother's pantry to grandmother's fading notebook to mother's typed cards to daughter's illustrated chapbook. Any dish evolves with each cook and each generation: cultures change, techniques develop, health concerns arise, a wider range of ingredients becomes available. And this is as it should be. Flavors, like folklore, are meant to be reinterpreted.

Many of my recipes have a long history and have traveled with me during forty years of wanderings through Iowa, Minnesota, Pennsylvania, and Missouri. Others come more recently from Washington state, California, Hawaii, Texas, New York, England, Ireland, and Japan. I have adjusted ingredients to make best use of our Pacific Northwest bounty, but I've also tried to remain true to the original spirit and flavor of each dish.

I hope you find the same joy in sampling these menus and recipes as I did in creating them.

KEEPING COLD FOODS COLD Immediately after preparing your cold picnic fare, refrigerate or freeze it for several hours until just before you leave for your picnic. Cooked sauces and dishes that will be served cold should be thoroughly heated before cooling and refrigeration. Bacteria grows in cool foods as well as hot foods. Keeping food at temperatures below 45°F is necessary to prevent the growth of organisms.

Pre-chill your insulated picnic chest or jug by filling it with ice water 30 minutes before packing. Transfer the chilled food directly to the drained, pre-chilled picnic chest in which you have also packed one of the following continuing sources of cold: water frozen in a cardboard milk carton and taped shut; frozen gel packs; or crushed ice secured in leakproof plastic bags.

Pack those foods most perishable (poultry, fish, meat, and dairy protein, and homemade sauces made with eggs) closest to the source of cold. Pack cold and hot foods in separate insulated picnic chests.

At the picnic site, place the chest in shade and do not open the lid more than absolutely necessary. Make a point not to bring home leftovers.

Wrap uncooked poultry, meat, and fish that you plan to grill later in heavy-duty foil and place in the picnic chest next to the source of cold. Pack your picnic chest as full as possible (while still allowing air circulation) with pre-chilled items. Distribute the gel packs or cartons of ice evenly.

KEEPING HOT FOODS HOT Cook hot picnic dishes as close to your picnic departure as possible. Heat each dish thoroughly, according to recipe directions. Preheat your insulated picnic chest or thermos by filling with boiling water 30 minutes before packing, then drain. Insulate your hot dishes immediately by one of the following methods: wrap hot container in foil and then in 8 to 10 layers of newspaper; wrap hot container in picnic blankets or tablecloths; or pack containers in an insulated picnic chest next to a wrapped tile or brick which you have heated in your oven.

Keep hot dishes together in one picnic carrier. Serve hot items as soon as possible after you arrive or reheat dishes over coals in a portable or park grill.

ABOUT RAW EGGS In recent years, there has been increasing concern about the presence of Salmonella in eggs. Once thought to contaminate only the shell, the bacteria has now been discovered in the white and yolk of the egg, transmitted from an infected hen before the eggshell forms. Over the last decade, Salmonella outbreaks, which began in the northeastern states, have spread farther south and west.

Unfortunately, there is no consensus as to the extent of the problem: it is unclear what percentage of eggs are contaminated and how many people are affected.

What we do know about Salmonella is that it can make you sick, and in immuno-suppressed persons, the elderly, the very young, or the unborn fetus, it can even be fatal. Salmonella multiplies rapidly at room temperature; therefore, careful packing of susceptible picnic foods is very important. Keep cold foods cold. The risk is lowered when eggs are kept refrigerated, cooked thoroughly, and served immediately. Discard any cracked eggs.

Salmonella bacteria are killed at 160°F, or when eggs are pasteurized (held at 140°F for 3 minutes). Pasteurized eggs are available in cartons at most supermarkets and can be substituted in recipes calling for raw, whole eggs. Acid—vinegar or lemon juice— is also said to kill the bacteria, though the precise amount of acid to add to a raw egg and how long this mixture should stand have not been determined.

We have included only a few raw-egg recipes in *Seattle Picnics* and caution our readers as follows: Because there is no clear knowl- edge as to the extent of the Salmonella problem, we all eat raw eggs at our own risk.

LOW-FAT, LOW-CHOLESTEROL SUBSTITUTIONS If you'd like to cut

the amounts of fat and cholesterol in your recipes, start by trimming all visible fat from beef, lamb, pork, and poultry (remove the skin from poultry, too). Next, try the following substitutions for dairy products, mayonnaise, and eggs.

If you decide simply to decrease the amount of a dairy fat in a recipe (rather than substituting for it), remember to add a little more liquid to the dish.

For cream cheese: Make yogurt cheese: Place 2 cups nonfat yogurt made without gelatin (Dannon brand, for example) in a cheese-cloth-lined colander; set over a bowl and let drain for 24 hours. Then cover and store in an opaque crock in the refrigerator until ready to use or for up to 2 weeks. Do not heat.

You may also use nonfat quark, available at Puget Consumers Co-op, Larry's Markets, and QFC. (This can be used in cooking.)

Or drain low-fat cottage cheese as directed for yogurt cheese; then beat with an electric mixer until smooth.

For sour cream: Drain and beat low-fat cottage cheese as directed above.

Or chill 1 can (12 ounces) evaporated low-fat milk until very cold, then whip with 1 teaspoon lemon juice until stiff.

You may also mix yogurt cheese (see directions above) with a little buttermilk.

For crème fraîche: Mix nonfat buttermilk with yogurt cheese (see directions above); or use yogurt cheese alone.

In place of crème fraîche as a dessert topping, use low-fat vanilla yogurt or low-fat plain yogurt flavored with undiluted orange or apple juice concentrate.

For half-and-half or whipping cream: In cold soups, use nonfat buttermilk (Foremost brand is available at Puget Consumers Co-op). Low-fat buttermilk can be warmed, but don't bring it to a boil. If you use it in a sauce or soup that will be cooked over high heat, stabilize it first by adding ½ teaspoon cornstarch to each ½ cup buttermilk.

For whipped cream: Prepare packaged dessert topping mix using skim milk.

For whipped cream as a dessert topping, use yogurt as suggested under "For crème fraîche" above.

For evaporated milk: Use evaporated low-fat milk.

For Cheddar cheese: Use a mixture of half Cheddar and half low-fat mozzarella cheese; or use one of the low-fat Cheddars now on the market.

For mayonnaise: Use a mixture of half low-fat yogurt and half reduced-calorie or cholesterol-free mayonnaise.

For whole eggs: For each whole egg, substitute 2 egg whites or ¼ cup Fleischmann's Egg Beaters™.

A Cherry Blossom Viewing for 8

Cold Steamed Asparagus
with
Hollandaise Sauce *
Minted Lamb in a Pocket *
Macadamia Nut Macaroons
Coffee

The Japanese have a wonderful tradition of turning out en masse each April to view the cherry blossoms. The fleeting, floating petals herald the passing of winter's cold and signify the transient nature of life. Because the trees are in their full glory so briefly, don't hesitate too long in planning your picnic. The University of Washington Liberal Arts Quadrangle and the Washington Park Arboretum are the best spots to enjoy a picnic under the cherry blossoms.

Along with the cherry blossoms, another signal that spring has arrived in the Northwest is the appearance of the first asparagus spears on local produce stands. The asparagus will remain green and tender if you steam the stalks no more than ten minutes before plunging them in cold water and packing them for your picnic.

HOLLANDAISE SAUCE

½ cup butter
3 egg yolks
2 tablespoons fresh lemon
juice
¼ teaspoon salt
Dash of white pepper
½ teaspoon prepared yellow
mustard

For years I had trouble making hollandaise sauce. It curdled. It separated. It didn't taste quite right. Then I discovered the secret: use the blender. You will make smooth, perfectly flavored hollandaise sauce from now on, I promise.

This recipe makes 1 cup of sauce — enough to top about 2 pounds of steamed asparagus. You can also use it as a dip for grilled shellfish.

In a small saucepan, heat butter until bubbly. Skim off and discard milk solids.

Place remaining ingredients in a blender; cover and blend for 5 seconds. With blender running, gradually drizzle in hot melted butter in a slow, steady stream until entirely absorbed.

Transport sauce to picnic site in a small thermos.

Makes about 1 cup (8 servings).

MINTED LAMB IN A POCKET

*1 leg of lamb (5 to 6
   pounds), boned and split
Salt to taste
Freshly ground black pepper
   to taste
3 cloves garlic, minced
Juice of 1 lemon
1 cup dry white wine
½ cup olive oil
¼ cup finely chopped fresh
   mint leaves
6 tablespoons butter, melted
Pita bread, warmed*

This is a more portable version of a dish I shared with my daughter in San Diego, during a long talk over Greek coffee with the owner of Niko's Greek Village. Grill the lamb at home before setting out for your picnic; or cook it at another picnic site where a charcoal grill is available.

———

Sprinkle lamb with salt and pepper, rub with garlic, and place in a large container. Combine lemon juice, wine, oil, mint, and butter; season to taste with pepper and pour over meat. Cover and refrigerate for at least 6 hours or overnight, turning meat over occasionally.

About 40 minutes before you are ready to eat, ignite coals and burn until white-hot. Drain meat; reserve marinade. Then open up meat and grill 3 inches from coals until done to your liking (about 20 minutes per side for medium). Heat marinade at side of grill; use to baste meat during grilling.

Cut meat diagonally into small, thin slices and use to fill warmed pita bread.

Makes 8 servings.

KENTUCKY DERBY DAY CELEBRATION
FOR 4

Grilled Trout or Catfish
with
Dill Sauce *
Tossed Green Salad
Corn Bread
Blueberry Barquettes *
Mint Juleps *
Orange Blossom Cooler *

Freshly caught, pan-fried trout and catfish are a vivid, pleasant memory from my childhood. My mouth still waters when I think of the sweet, distinctive flakes of catfish on my tongue. As fond as I am of seafood, I've not found any I crave quite as much or as often as that ugly Mississippi River fish.

Wrap the fish in foil so you won't lose any of its juices and add just a tad of the Dill Sauce. The wonderful, succulent flavor of the fish should rule.

With this menu on the picnic table, you will need only one or two additions to create a completely successful Derby Day celebration: a portable TV or radio for following the race, and at least one guest skilled at setting the odds for your own private wager. You might want to select a color scheme that duplicates your favorite jockey's silks.

DILL SAUCE

1½ tablespoons butter
2 shallots, minced
1 teaspoon all-purpose flour
¼ cup dry white wine
¼ cup dry vermouth
2 tablespoons champagne
   vinegar
¼ cup half-and-half
½ teaspoon snipped fresh dill
Salt and freshly ground black
   pepper to taste

A rich, versatile sauce—perfect over trout, catfish, grilled halibut cheeks, or salmon. I like to spoon only 2 tablespoons or so of sauce over each serving, but the recipe makes enough for those who like to top their fish more lavishly.

———

In a medium saucepan, melt butter. Add shallots and sauté until soft. Add flour; stir until blended. Add wine, vermouth, vinegar, half-and-half, and dill. Stir until bubbly and well blended. Season with salt and pepper.

Transport sauce to picnic site in a small thermos.

Makes about 1 cup (4 to 8 servings).

BLUEBERRY BARQUETTES

*Barquette Shells (recipe
  follows)*
⅓ cup milk
1½ tablespoons cornstarch
½ cup half-and-half
⅓ cup sugar
2 egg yolks, lightly beaten
¾ teaspoon vanilla
2 tablespoons cornstarch
¼ cup water
½ cup sugar
*2½ cups fresh blueberries,
  rinsed and drained*
8 mint sprigs

In keeping with the racing theme, you might call these boat-shaped tarts "bluegrass barquettes"—but they are topped with plump Northwest blueberries, not Kentucky bluegrass. Every bite oozes creamy custard and juicy berries.

You can make both the custard and the Barquette Shells the day before the picnic. Barquette molds in several sizes are available at local kitchenware shops.

———

Prepare Barquette Shells.

Next, prepare custard: In a bowl, combine milk and 1½ tablespoons cornstarch; set aside. In a small saucepan, combine half-and-half and ⅓ cup sugar; bring to a boil. Reduce heat to low and gradually stir in milk-cornstarch mixture. Cook, stirring constantly, until thickened. Remove from heat.

Beat a small amount of the hot cornstarch mixture into egg yolks; then return egg yolk mixture to saucepan. Return to low heat and cook until heated through and slightly thicker (about 10 more minutes), stirring constantly. Do not overcook. Remove from heat and stir in vanilla.

Pour custard into a small bowl; cover with plastic wrap, laying it directly on surface of custard to prevent a film from forming. Refrigerate for 1 hour or until completely cold.

Meanwhile, prepare glaze: In a saucepan, dissolve 2 tablespoons cornstarch in water. Mix in ½ cup sugar and 1 cup of the blueberries. Bring to a boil; then reduce heat and simmer, uncovered, until thickened (about 10 minutes), mashing berries as you stir to create a sauce. Strain and cool.

To assemble barquettes, spread each shell with a thin lining of glaze; add a layer of cooled custard. Top each barquette with 3 tablespoons of the remaining blueberries, then cover with remaining glaze. Garnish each barquette with a mint sprig.

Make 8 barquettes (4 servings).

BARQUETTE SHELLS
1 cup all-purpose flour
½ teaspoon salt
1½ teaspoons sugar
¼ cup cold unsalted butter
1 egg yolk
3 tablespoons ice water
Sugar

In a medium bowl, mix flour, salt, and 1½ teaspoons sugar. Cut in butter with a pastry cutter until mixture resembles coarse meal. Mix in egg yolk. Stir in ice water and gather pastry into a ball. Flatten into a disk, wrap in plastic wrap, and refrigerate for 1 hour.

Roll out pastry between 2 sheets of wax paper to a thickness of ⅛ inch. Cut out with a 6-inch-long fluted oval cookie cutter (or cut into ovals with a sharp knife). Use ovals to line 8 oval barquette molds (each about 4¾ inches long by 2 inches wide); prick bottoms of shells with a fork. Sprinkle with sugar. Freeze for 10 minutes. Meanwhile, preheat oven to 375°F.

Line frozen pastry shells with foil, then fill with dried beans or aluminum pie weights. Bake in preheated oven until lightly browned at edges (about 20 minutes). Remove pie weights and foil; continue to bake shells until golden brown (10 to 15 more minutes). Cool slightly, then remove from pans. If made in advance, cover airtight until ready to use.

MINT JULEPS

4 fresh catnip leaves
Crushed ice
1½ cups whiskey
2 tablespoons plus
   2 teaspoons sugar
   dissolved in 2 cups water
8 catnip sprigs

A very opinionated world traveler tells me that true juleps are made with catnip, not spearmint—but he can't explain why the name isn't "catnip julep"! Never mind, the controversy adds to the flavor of the drink as well as to its mystique.

Since you'll want all your guests to enjoy their juleps at the same time, appoint one of them your assistant bartender.

———

To make each julep, hold a catnip leaf inside an 8- to 10-ounce glass and tear it or bruise it with a spoon. Fill glass with crushed ice. Cover ice with 6 tablespoons of the whiskey, then pour a fourth of the sugar-water mixture over whiskey. Tear leaves of 2 catnip sprigs to release their essence; then poke sprigs into glass. Repeat to prepare remaining drinks. Sip slowly.

Makes 4 servings.

ORANGE BLOSSOM COOLER

⅓ cup (half of a 6-ounce can)
   frozen orange juice
   concentrate
¼ cup sugar
½ cup milk
½ teaspoon vanilla
5 or 6 ice cubes
4 mint sprigs

As creamy and smooth as a citrusy Dreamsicle™.

———

Combine all ingredients except mint sprigs in a blender. Blend until smooth. Pour into a 1-quart thermos for transport to picnic site. Shake well before pouring into glasses; garnish each serving with a mint sprig.

Makes 4 servings.

OPENING DAY OUTING FOR 8

Crudité Platter
with
Vegetable Dip *
Barbecued Chicken
Cheese Bread
Marbled Brownies
Sparkling Burgundy
or
Puerto Rican Coquito *
Peach Fizz *

This menu features plenty of portable finger food, the better to transfer your meal easily from shore to dinghy to sailboat. Everything can be prepared prior to the picnic; come opening day, you can just relax on deck, waiting to catch sight of the first billowing spinnaker coming through the Montlake Cut.

VEGETABLE DIP

2 cups low-fat cottage cheese
1 cup mayonnaise,
    commercial or homemade
    (recipe follows)
2 tablespoons fresh lemon
    juice
4 tablespoons green onion,
    minced
2 tablespoons Dijon mustard
4 teaspoons fresh herbs,
    snipped
Salt and freshly ground

Serve as a dip for sliced tart apples or vegetables.

——

In a blender, combine all ingredients and blend thoroughly until smooth. Cover and refrigerate until ready to transport to picnic.

Makes about 2 cups (8 servings).

BLENDER MAYONNAISE
1 egg, room temperature
2 tablespoons white wine vinegar
¾ teaspoon salt
½ teaspoon dry mustard
¼ teaspoon paprika
½ teaspoon fresh herbs, snipped
    (chives, thyme, chervil, basil, marjoram,
    or tarragon)
1 cup olive or vegetable oil

For those who like all their ingredients absolutely fresh.

———

In a blender, combine all ingredients except oil. Blend until smooth.

With blender running, gradually drizzle in oil in a slow, steady stream until entirely absorbed. Cover and refrigerate until ready to use or for up to 2 weeks.

Makes about 1 cup.

PUERTO RICAN COQUITO

4 egg yolks
1½ tablespoons sugar
1 cup canned coconut milk
1 can (14 ounces) sweetened
  condensed milk
1 teaspoon vanilla
1 cup plus 2 tablespoons
  Puerto Rican white rum
Ground cinnamon

A rich, creamy, refreshing cooler.

——

In a bowl, beat egg yolks and sugar until frothy. Beat in coconut milk and condensed milk, then stir in vanilla and rum. Cover and refrigerate for at least 1 hour or up to 3 days. Transport to picnic site in a large thermos; shake well before serving. Pour into small glasses; sprinkle with cinnamon.

Makes 8 servings.

PEACH FIZZ

1 quart peach nectar
1 tray (about 16) ice cubes
2 cups seltzer water, chilled
Crushed ice
8 mint sprigs

A drink that appeals to all the senses.

———

In a large insulated picnic jug, mix peach nectar and ice cubes. Transport to picnic site. Add seltzer water just before serving; pour into ice-filled glasses and garnish with mint sprigs.

Makes 8 servings.

Spring Moonrise Rendezvous for 8

Ceviche on Bibb Lettuce *
Fusilli with Lemon Pesto Sauce *
Italian Bread
Strawberry Mascarpone Gratin *
Wine
Spring Fever Cure *

When you choose this menu, nothing will distract you from watching the full moon rise above Seattle's magnificent skyline: each dish can be prepared before you leave for your picnic, giving you plenty of time to get settled at one of the area's prime moon-viewing spots.

You will need to pick a place that has an unimpeded view of the east, of course. Gas Works Park, Madrona Park, South Seattle Community College Arboretum, Kubota Garden, Luther Burbank Park, Seattle University campus, or a Washington State ferry are all wonderful possibilities.

Whichever you choose, enhance the night's spell by sharing a generous platter of tiny lime-tenderized scallops. They will whet your appetite for the forkfuls of Italian pasta to follow.

CEVICHE ON BIBB LETTUCE

2 pounds bay scallops, rinsed,
  drained, and chopped
½ cup fresh or bottled
  grapefruit juice
½ cup fresh or bottled lime
  juice
½ teaspoon hot pepper sauce
2 scallions, sliced
1 small red bell pepper, seeded
  and chopped
1 tablespoon chopped fresh
  cilantro
Bibb lettuce leaves

The citrus juices in this recipe actually "cook" the scallops by acting on the protein in the shellfish. The process takes time, though, so be sure to start your ceviche marinating at least 12 hours before serving. The results are well worth the wait.

———

In a large glass bowl, combine all ingredients except lettuce. Cover and refrigerate until scallops are opaque (about 12 hours) or for up to 2 days. Just before serving, drain; then serve on lettuce leaves.

Makes 8 servings.

FUSILLI WITH LEMON PESTO SAUCE

*2 cups fresh basil leaves
(1 ounce), rinsed, patted
dry, and chopped*
4 teaspoons sesame oil
*6 tablespoons fresh lemon
juice*
¼ cup soy sauce
*2 teaspoons grated fresh
gingerroot or 4 teaspoons
finely chopped fresh ginger
shoots*
2 teaspoons sugar
*2 packages (about 10 ounces
each) fresh fusilli
(corkscrew pasta)*

If you like, top this pasta dish with marinated cooked shellfish.

———

In a blender, combine basil with oil. Blend until puréed. With blender running, add remaining ingredients except fusilli; blend until smooth. Pour sauce into a thermos; refrigerate until picnic day or for up to 1 week. Bring sauce to room temperature before you leave for the picnic.

Following package directions, cook fusilli; drain well. Place in a container, cover, and wrap in newspapers to transport to picnic site.

To serve, pour sauce over hot pasta; toss to mix.

Makes 8 servings.

STRAWBERRY MASCARPONE GRATIN

3 eggs
3 cups fresh strawberries,
   rinsed, hulled, and sliced
4½ tablespoons sugar
3 tablespoons fresh lemon
   juice
¾ cup mascarpone cheese,
   softened
6 tablespoons sugar
6 tablespoons sweet marsala
   wine

Enjoy hot, juicy fresh strawberries under a melting cloud of bronzed Italian cream cheese. Baking this delectable dessert in individual custard cups makes it easier to transport to the picnic site. (If you cannot find mascarpone, substitute regular cream cheese.)

———

Remove eggs from refrigerator and bring to room temperature; then separate and set aside.

In a bowl, mix strawberries with 4½ tablespoons sugar; set aside. In a clean bowl, beat egg whites until stiff. Set aside. In a third bowl, beat lemon juice into softened mascarpone cheese; set aside.

Preheat oven to 350°F. In the top of a double boiler, combine egg yolks, 6 tablespoons sugar, and wine. Set over simmering water and beat with an electric mixer until foamy and very thick (5 to 7 minutes). Do not overcook.

Add a little of the hot egg yolk mixture to egg whites, then fold in remaining egg whites. Divide equally among 8 oven-proof ¾-cup custard cups. Top evenly with strawberries, then top each cup with 2 or 3 spoonfuls of the lemon-cheese mixture. Set custard cups in a baking dish; pour hot water around custard cups to 1-inch level.

Bake in preheated oven for 20 minutes. Then turn oven to broil; brown tops of desserts (about 5 minutes). Wrap in foil or newspapers and transport to picnic site. Don't forget to bring spoons.

Makes 8 servings.

SPRING FEVER CURE

⅓ cup *sugar*
⅔ cup *water*
¼ cup *fresh lemon juice*
½ cup *fresh orange juice*
¼ cup *minced fresh mint*
¼ cup *minced fresh lemon*
  balm
2 quarts *ginger ale, chilled*
8 lemon balm *sprigs*
½ cup *Crème Fraîche (recipe*
  on page 103)

If ever a drink was a spring tonic, this is it. The combination of mint and citrus, popular in one form or another since medieval times, provides the perfect medicine for winter melancholy.

———

In a saucepan, combine sugar and water; bring to a boil, then boil, stirring occasionally, until reduced to ¼ cup syrup (about 20 minutes). Add lemon juice and orange juice. Remove from heat, add mint and minced lemon balm, cover, and let steep for 1 hour. Strain through a fine sieve or cheesecloth. Transport to picnic site in a thermos.

Before serving, mix syrup with ginger ale. Pour into glasses; garnish each with a sprig of lemon balm and top with a dollop of crème fraîche.

Makes 8 servings.

MAIWEIN FEST FOR 8

Skewered Tortellini in Sun-dried Tomato Sauce
Grilled Baby Vegetables
Cheese Puffs
*Tirami Su**
*Maibowle**
*Apple Tea**

Before this traditional European country festival can begin, handfuls of sweet woodruff blossoms need to be gathered for the Maibowle, a refreshing spring drink. Their blooming and the first day of May coincide and have long been associated with spring, for when the odor of the leaves is released, the smell of new-mown hay fills the air. Although Mai Fest is a German celebration, Italian foods perfectly complement the Maibowle and add color, texture, and flavor to the menu.

For the Skewered Tortellini, simply purchase a package of dry tortellini and a jar of sun-dried tomato sauce at your favorite market. Prepare the pasta according to package directions and drain; then smother with sauce, thread on 6-inch bamboo skewers, and heat on the grill. (Remember to soak the skewers in water for at least 20 minutes before using them.)

For the baby vegetables, try tiny eggplants, beets, small pattypan squash, or miniature ears of corn.

Tirami Su

¾ cup plus 2 tablespoons
    double espresso coffee
½ cup coffee-flavored liqueur
    or white crème de cacao
12 ladyfingers (3-ounce
    package)
1 cup whipping cream
2 egg yolks
2 tablespoons sugar
1 cup mascarpone cheese,
    softened
Unsweetened cocoa powder
White chocolate leaves
    (optional)

The sophisticated look of this rich, memorable dessert will fool your guests into thinking you spent hours in preparation. The name *tirami su* means "pick-me-up" — perhaps in reference to the generous amount of espresso coffee that goes into the dish.

———

In a bowl, mix coffee and liqueur. Split ladyfingers; dip in coffee mixture and set aside.

In a chilled bowl, beat cream until stiff. Set aside.

In another bowl, beat egg yolks and sugar until thick and lemon-colored; slowly beat in softened mascarpone cheese. Fold whipped cream into cheese mixture.

In a 9-by-13-inch glass dish, alternate layers of cheese mixture and ladyfingers, finishing with a layer of cheese mixture. Dust with cocoa. Decorate with white chocolate leaves, if desired.

Keep covered and cool until time to serve. If prepared in advance, refrigerate for up to 2 days.

Makes 8 to 12 servings.

NOTE: If you like, prepare an extra package of ladyfingers and place them upright around edge of dish. Strong regular coffee may be used in place of espresso. Neufchâtel cheese or nonfat quark may be substituted for mascarpone cheese; 1 package whipped topping mix prepared with skim milk may be substituted for whipped cream.

Maibowle

(Waldmeister Bowl, Maiwein)

2 bunches sweet woodruff
leaves (about 20 leaves)
2 bunches sweet woodruff
blossoms (about 10
sprigs) or 1 small muslin
bag dried woodruff
2 cups fresh strawberries
½ cup sugar
½ cup cognac or brandy
3 bottles (750 ml. each)
young, fruity white wine,
such as Riesling, Moselle,
or Rhine
1 bottle (750 ml.)
champagne

Drinking Maibowle is a German rite of spring, honored throughout the country as a springtime tonic. The punch is made with the tiny white blossoms of the wild sweet woodruff (*Galium odoratum*, sometimes also sold as *Asperula odorata*), a creeping herb that blooms in May. Both seeds and plants of sweet woodruff are sold at local nurseries and herb farms. If you'd like to sample Maiwein but don't want to make it yourself, you can purchase a Northwest May Wine from Latah Creek Wine Cellars. Very rarely, imported German Maiwein is available from some wine merchants.

Rinse woodruff leaves and blossoms and spin dry in a salad spinner. Rinse 12 whole strawberries for an ice ring; then prepare an ice ring small enough to fit inside your punch bowl, using a few woodruff leaves, blossoms, and the 12 whole strawberries. Freeze.

Place remaining woodruff leaves and blossoms in a deep bowl. Add sugar, cognac or brandy, and 1 bottle of the wine. Cover and let stand overnight at room temperature. Refrigerate remaining wine and champagne.

The next day, strain woodruff mixture through a sieve or cheese-cloth and pour into a thermos. Rinse, hull, and slice remaining strawberries. Transport strained woodruff mixture, sliced straw-berries, chilled wine and champagne, and ice ring to picnic. At the picnic site, place ice ring in punch bowl; pour woodruff mixture, wine, and champagne over ice ring and add strawberries.

Makes 8 servings.

APPLE TEA

1 quart water
6 tea bags (apple or lemon
tea is especially good)
2 cups apple juice
½ cup fresh lemon juice
Crushed ice
Sugar to taste
8 mint sprigs

This refreshing drink can be served either iced or hot.

———

In a small saucepan, bring water to a boil. Place tea bags in a teapot; pour boiling water over tea bags and let steep for 3 minutes. Remove tea bags; let tea stand at room temperature until you are ready to leave for picnic. Then pour tea, apple juice, and lemon juice into a 2-quart thermos and transport to picnic site.

To serve, pour into ice-filled glasses. Sweeten to taste with sugar and garnish with mint sprigs.

Makes 8 servings.

Bastille Day Celebration for 8

Brie and Crackers
Grilled Halibut Cheeks
with
Champagne Caper Sauce *
Asparagus Vinaigrette *
French Bread
Tricolor Berry Tart in Gingersnap Crust *
Champagne
Sparkling Grape Juice

Join Seattle's French expatriates in commemorating the capture of the Bastille on July 14. At the same time, raise a glass to the culture that has done so much to share with us its passion for fresh, simple food.

Brie, champagne, vinaigrette, a crusty loaf, and berry tarts are among the best of those simple taste pleasures. So easily obtained, prepared, and enjoyed, it's as if the French created these especially for a Northwest picnic.

CHAMPAGNE CAPER SAUCE

2 tablespoons capers, rinsed
and drained
1¼ cups champagne
2 teaspoons cornstarch
1 tablespoon water
1 tablespoon butter
Salt and freshly ground
black pepper to taste

Capers—the pickled unopened buds of a spiny shrub—add a Mediterranean accent and lively flavor to this sauce. It may be prepared ahead of time, then drizzled over grilled halibut cheeks at the picnic site. (The recipe makes enough for about 2 pounds of fish.)

In a saucepan, combine capers and 1 cup of the champagne. Bring to a simmer; then simmer for 10 minutes. Stir together cornstarch and water; slowly stir into heated champagne. Cook over low heat, stirring constantly, until smooth and thickened. Add butter and stir until melted. Stir in remaining ¼ cup champagne. Cook, stirring, for 2 more minutes. Season with salt and pepper.

Transport sauce to picnic site in a small thermos.

Makes about 1 cup (8 servings).

ASPARAGUS VINAIGRETTE

*2½ pounds thin, tender fresh
  asparagus*
⅔ cup olive oil
½ cup white wine vinegar
½ teaspoon Dijon mustard
½ teaspoon salt
*⅛ teaspoon freshly ground
  black pepper*
*1 tablespoon chopped fresh
  tarragon*
1 tablespoon chopped scallion

Asparagus is a truly versatile vegetable. Steamed, then marinated in vinaigrette dressing, it can appear at your picnic as is, or can be added to salads.

When you make this dish, be sure to allow at least 2 hours for the asparagus to marinate.

———

Wash and trim asparagus, then steam over boiling water just until tender (about 10 minutes). Drain, rinse with cold water, and drain again. Arrange in a glass dish. Combine remaining ingredients in a screw-top glass jar; cover tightly, shake well, and pour over asparagus. Cover and refrigerate for at least 2 hours before picnic time or for up to 1 week.

Makes 8 servings.

TRICOLOR BERRY TART
IN GINGERSNAP CRUST

*1 box (7 ounces) Finnish
gingersnaps, crushed*
¼ cup finely chopped nuts
⅓ cup butter, melted
1 envelope unflavored gelatin
*1¾ cups unsweetened white
grape juice*
*1 cup each fresh gooseberries
or white grapes, blue-
berries, and strawberries,
rinsed and drained*

Top this tart with berries that match the three colors of the French flag—red strawberries, blueberries, and white strawberries. If white strawberries are unavailable, use gooseberries or seedless green grapes instead.

Finnish gingersnaps are preferred. Other comparable gingersnaps may be substituted.

———

Preheat oven to 375°F. In a bowl, mix crushed gingersnaps and nuts. Add butter and mix well. Press mixture firmly up sides and over bottom of a 9-inch pie pan. Bake in preheated oven for 5 minutes. Cool.

Meanwhile, prepare glaze: In a medium saucepan, soften gelatin in grape juice for 5 minutes. Then heat over low heat, stirring, until gelatin is dissolved. Remove from heat and set aside until ready to use.

To assemble, fill tart shell with gooseberries, blueberries, and strawberries. Brush prepared glaze over fruit. Refrigerate until glaze is set (about 30 minutes).

Makes 8 servings.

Tokyo Summer Grill for 5

Pickled Vegetables
Yakitori (Chicken Shish Kabob) ∗
or
Okonomi-yaki (Japanese Pizzas or "Cook to Taste" Pancakes) ∗
Momo-kan (Jellied Peach Cubes) ∗
Homebrewed Sake ∗
Kirin Beer
Calpico

The best way to discover Japan's favorite summertime foods is to walk through a busy Tokyo neighborhood. Food carts and open-air restaurants are everywhere. When you turn a corner and encounter the pungent, heady aroma of grilled chicken or the spicy-sweet smoke of the okonomi-yaki hot plate, you won't be able to resist stepping beneath the *noren* (the short, indigo-colored curtains that tell you a shop is open) flapping over the restaurant door.

Seattle's Asian markets carry a wide variety of Japanese fresh foods and seasonings, as well as bottles of *Calpico* (known in Japan as *Calpis*), Japan's favorite thirst-quencher. It's a sweet, milky, slightly fermented drink; you buy it as a concentrate, then reconstitute it with chilled seltzer water.

YAKITORI

(CHICKEN SHISH KABOB)

Yakitori no Tare (Yakitori Sauce), recipe follows
1 whole chicken breast, skinned, boned, split, and cut into 2-inch squares
2 chicken thighs, skinned, boned, and cut into 2-inch squares
2 bell peppers (any color), seeded and cut into 2-inch chunks
1 baby eggplant, cut into 2-inch chunks
12 shiitake mushroom caps, brushed and cut into halves or thirds
3 negi (spring scallions) or regular scallions, cut into 2-inch pieces
Toppings: Grated fresh gingerroot and shichimi togarishi (seven tastes pepper)

Yakitori is probably one of the easiest Japanese dishes to adapt to an outdoor picnic grill—and enjoying these succulent morsels of chicken and vegetables is one of Japan's favorite pastimes.

———

Prepare sauce.

About 40 minutes before you are ready to eat, ignite coals and burn until white-hot. Meanwhile, soak twenty 10-inch bamboo skewers in water for 20 minutes. Then thread chicken, bell peppers, eggplant, mushrooms, and scallions equally onto skewers. Dip each skewer into jar of sauce; or brush sauce over skewers.

When coals are ready, grill skewers 3 inches from coals just until chicken is cooked through and vegetables are tender (2 to 3 minutes per side). Serve with a sprinkling of grated ginger and shichimi togarishi. Have plenty of sake and Kirin beer available just in case you overdo it with the seasonings.

Makes 5 servings.

YAKITORI NO TARE
¼ cup sake
1 tablespoon all-purpose flour
¾ cup soy sauce
⅓ cup sugar

In a bowl, combine sake and flour to make a paste. In a small saucepan, mix soy sauce and sugar; then stir in flour paste. Cook over low heat, stirring constantly, until sugar is dissolved and sauce is thickened (about 10 minutes). Remove from heat. Pour into a tall, narrow jar. Refrigerate until you are ready to leave for the picnic.

Makes ½ cup.

OKONOMI-YAKI

(JAPANESE PIZZAS OR "COOK TO TASTE" PANCAKES)

2 cups all-purpose flour
½ teaspoon baking powder
⅛ teaspoon salt
½ head cabbage, chopped
4 eggs
8 raw shrimp (½ pound total),
*   shelled, deveined, and cut into*
*   strips*
½ pound squid, cleaned, skinned,
*   and cut into strips*
¼ cup tenkasu (deep-fried
*   tempura batter) crumbs*
2 tablespoons vegetable oil
10 ounces lean pork, cut into thin
*   strips*
2 tablespoons minced beni-shoga
*   (red pickled ginger)*
Okonomi-yaki sauce
Mayonnaise, commercial or
*   homemade (recipe on page 31)*
Dried ko-gatsuo (bonito) powder
*   or flakes*
Dried ao-nori (green seaweed)
*   flakes*
Karashi (hot yellow mustard) or
*   any mustard that is not sweet*
*   or vinegary*

Okonomi-yaki are prepared like pancakes and look like pancakes—but because they are savory, they're really more pizzas than pancakes. And like Americans, the Japanese love to personalize their "pizza" toppings. The choices listed here are the traditional ones.

Once you have the technique down, you'll find okonomi-yaki quick to prepare. Make them at home before leaving for your picnic.

Okonomi-yaki sauce and other ingredients are available at local Asian food markets.

———

In a large bowl, combine flour, baking powder, and salt. Stir in cabbage. Add eggs, one at a time, beating well after each addition. Add shrimp, squid, and tenkasu. Mix well.

Coat a hot frying pan or griddle with some of the oil. Add a fifth of the pork strips and sauté until browned; then reduce heat and pour a fifth of the pancake batter over pork. Top evenly with a fifth of the ginger and cook until browned on bottom, then flip over and brown top. Remove from pan. Repeat to cook 4 more pancakes, re-oiling griddle as needed and using remaining pork, batter, and ginger.

Brush each pancake with a layer of okonomi-yaki sauce and mayonnaise; then sprinkle with bonito and ao-nori flakes. Serve, folded over, with mustard.

Makes 5 servings.

MOMO-KAN

(JELLIED PEACH CUBES)

*1 kanten (agar-agar) strip
    (0.2 ounce)*
Water
1 cup sugar
*¾ cup peeled, mashed fresh
    peaches*
1 teaspoon fresh lemon juice
*Miniature rice-paste or
    sugar-paste shapes, such
    as fish or blossoms (you'll
    need about 16)*

These clear, slightly sweet jellied cubes, made from agar-agar (a type of algae), are a favorite summer cooler. The Japanese delight in placing elaborate rice-paste or sugar-paste shapes in the middle of each cube; every shop seems to have its own signature design. You might try your hand at fashioning tiny Japanese carp or pale pink cherry blossoms.

Momo-kan do not melt and may be prepared ahead of time.

———

Soak kanten strip in water for 30 minutes. Squeeze out water; tear strip into small pieces. Rinse with cold water, then squeeze dry again. Place kanten in a small saucepan, add 2 cups water, and bring to a boil; boil, stirring, until kanten is dissolved. Add sugar and simmer until dissolved. Pour through a sieve into a bowl.

Mash peaches and lemon juice together into a pulp; press peach mixture through a sieve into kanten mixture. Stir. Pour into an 8-inch-square dish or pan over rice-paste or sugar-paste shapes. Refrigerate until set (about 2 hours) or overnight. Cut into 2-inch squares.

Makes 16 squares (about 5 servings).

HOMEBREWED SAKE

2¼ pounds ordinary raw rice
  (not instant or precooked)
6 quarts warm water
1½ envelopes active dry yeast
2 boxes (15 ounces each)
  raisins
4 pounds (about 9½ cups)
  sugar
2 oranges, cut into eighths

This recipe has been in my collection since the early sixties, when it was given to me by a canoeing companion. At the time, I didn't realize how rare it was. Recently, I requested a homebrew recipe for sake during a trip to Japan—only to learn that making sake at home is illegal there!

On my return, I read every homebrew book I could find and discovered just one reference to homebrewed sake: mention of a man in Iowa who has successfully made his own sake for years. With this recipe, you too will be able to join an elite group of sake homebrewers.

Sake may be consumed immediately after it's made. In summer, drink it at room temperature or cool; in winter, gently heat it in its bottle in a saucepan of water. Serve cool sake in crystal sake cups or in *masu* (square wooden sake cups) with a pinch of salt on the edge; offer warm sake in tiny china sake cups.

———

In a 2½- to 3-gallon crock or picnic jug, combine all ingredients. Let stand for 3 weeks, stirring every fifth day. Strain through a large sieve and bottle in 8 sterilized 1-quart bottles. Cork. Sake will keep for up to 6 months.

Makes 2 gallons.

BAVARIAN BRATWURST AND BEER BASH
FOR 12

Bratwurst and Sauerkraut
Kaiser Rolls
Mustard
Sliced Tomatoes
Roasted Herbed Corn in the Husk
Grandma Holz's Warm German Potato Salad ★
Nut Strudel ★
Sunbrewed Iced Tea
German Beer

I can close my eyes and instantly recapture the mouth-watering sensations of my last Wisconsin bratwurst feed. Plump, savory sausages smoking and crackling on the huge grills, ready for a squeeze of mustard and a mound of sauerkraut. Mountains of ears of white, tender sweet corn steamed in the coals in their wet husks, then shucked and dipped in 5-pound tins of melted butter. Piles of sliced sun-ripened, juicy beefsteak tomatoes, scoops of warm potato salad—and all of it washed down with mugs of ice-cold stout. Ahhh, the Midwest Germans—they know how to throw a picnic!

GRANDMA HOLZ'S
WARM GERMAN POTATO SALAD

4 pounds red new potatoes, scrubbed

6 slices bacon, cut up with scissors

1 small onion, minced

1 tablespoon all-purpose flour

½ cup cider vinegar

½ cup water

Salt to taste

1 tablespoon sugar, or to taste

2 tablespoons chopped parsley or fresh dill

In the Midwest, no picnic is complete without German potato salad. Traditionally, it is served warm.

———

Place unpeeled whole potatoes in a large saucepan. Cover with water. Bring to a boil; reduce heat, cover, and simmer until potatoes are tender (about 20 minutes).

While potatoes are cooking, prepare dressing. In a frying pan, cook bacon pieces over medium heat until lightly browned and crisp. Remove with a slotted metal spoon and drain on paper towels. Add onion to bacon drippings; sauté until lightly browned. Add flour; stir to blend well. Stir in vinegar and water. Cook over low heat for 1 minute, then add cooked bacon pieces. Season to taste with salt and sugar. Remove from heat.

Drain potatoes; peel and slice into a large bowl. Pour dressing over potatoes and mix gently. Wrap in newspapers to keep warm; transport to picnic. For best flavor, let salad stand for at least 2 hours. Sprinkle with parsley or dill before serving.

Makes 12 servings.

NUT STRUDEL

5 cups sifted all-purpose flour
5 tablespoons gluten flour
3 eggs, well beaten
½ cup butter, melted
3½ tablespoons sugar
½ teaspoon salt
4 drops white vinegar
1½ cups lukewarm water
Vegetable oil
Nut Filling (recipe follows)
Unsweetened whipped cream
*   or Clotted Cream (recipe*
*   on page 111)*

At a gathering not long ago, one of the guests told me she had never tasted anything quite so wonderful as nut strudel, but was continually frustrated in her efforts to find a source in Seattle. Intrigued, I set out to create a recipe.

————

Place all-purpose flour in a mound on large pastry board or flat surface. Make a well in center; fill well with gluten flour, eggs, ¼ cup of the butter, sugar, salt, vinegar, and water. Mix by hand until dough forms a tight ball. Rub top of ball with oil, cover with a warm, damp towel, and let rest for 30 minutes.

Cover a large, sturdy table (at least 4 feet square) with a clean floured cloth. Slowly, carefully work and pull dough until it is paper-thin. Trim thick ends, then let dough dry for about 30 minutes. Meanwhile, prepare Nut Filling.

Preheat oven to 400°F. Grease a large baking sheet. Brush dough with some of the remaining ¼ cup melted butter. Fold dough in half, then in half again, forming a 4-layer rectangle; butter each layer. Spread with Nut Filling and roll up like a jelly roll, starting from a long side.

Place roll on prepared baking sheet. If roll is too long for your baking sheet (it probably will be), curve it into a U-shape or cut it in half. Bake in preheated oven until golden brown (about 30 minutes), brushing every 15 minutes with melted butter. Cut into slices and wrap in foil for transport to picnic site. Serve warm, with dollops of unsweetened whipped cream or Clotted Cream.

Makes 12 servings.

NUT FILLING
½ cup milk
¾ pound skinned hazelnuts, blanched almonds, or pecans, finely chopped
1 cup sugar
Pinch of salt
Grated peel of ½ lemon
½ cup peeled, grated apple

In a small saucepan, scald milk. Place nuts in a bowl; pour in milk, then add remaining ingredients and mix well.

BEACH BERRY BINGO FOR 6

Grilled Salmon Sausages *
Spinach Salad with Strawberries *
French Rolls
Berries and Nuts Dipped in White Chocolate
Frozen Strawberries and Raspberries in Champagne
or
Heat-squelcher Punch *

Summertime in Washington is berry-picking time. And what better way to celebrate the lengthy berry season than with a beach party? This menu presents fresh berries in four creative ways; use your imagination to come up with more.

To make the dessert, dip your choice of berries in melted white chocolate at home, then place them in foil petit-four cups and pass them around in a fancy candy box at the picnic. Strawberries, raspberries, blueberries, and huckleberries are all delicious prepared this way.

You need only two or three frozen berries for each glass of champagne; in the sun, they'll sparkle like jewels in your glass.

SALMON SAUSAGES

1 large egg
2 tablespoons mirin (sweet
rice wine)
2 tablespoons fresh lemon
juice
½ teaspoon salt
½ teaspoon white pepper
Large pinch of cayenne
pepper
1 pound raw salmon,
skinned, boned, and cut up
¼ cup whipping cream
¼ pound smoked salmon,
chopped
¼ pound raw shrimp, shelled,
deveined, and cubed
1 tablespoon snipped fresh dill
1 teaspoon snipped fresh chives

Grill these sausages, or split and serve cold for a salmon sausage sandwich.

———

Bring a large kettle of water to a boil. Meanwhile, in a small bowl, beat together egg, wine, lemon juice, salt, white pepper, and cayenne. In a food processor, purée raw salmon. With processor running, slowly add egg mixture. Process until smoothly puréed.

In a chilled bowl, beat cream until stiff. Fold into salmon mixture. Add smoked salmon, shrimp, dill, and chives. Place a sixth of the mixture on a buttered sheet of foil and shape into a 1½ inch-thick roll, enclosing and compressing in foil. Twist ends to seal. Repeat to shape 5 more sausages.

Reduce heat under kettle of boiling water. Drop in sausages and poach for 20 minutes. Remove carefully. Cool; then refrigerate until picnic time or for up to 3 days. Do not freeze.

If desired, split sausages and grill until browned before serving.

Makes 6 servings.

SPINACH SALAD WITH STRAWBERRIES

*2 bunches fresh spinach,
washed and trimmed*
¼ cup sugar
1 egg yolk
*3 tablespoons fresh lemon
juice*
*6 tablespoons nut or vegetable
oil*
*2 cups fresh strawberries,
rinsed, hulled, and sliced*
*½ cup slivered almonds,
toasted*

This beautiful salad is often the hit of the menu at my sister Carolyn's picnics.

———

Tear spinach leaves into bite-size pieces. In a small bowl, mix sugar, egg yolk, lemon juice, and oil; whisk briskly. Transport spinach, salad dressing, strawberries, and almonds in separate covered containers to picnic.

At the picnic site, combine spinach and strawberries and toss gently. Drizzle dressing sparingly over salad just before serving. Top with almonds.

Makes 6 servings.

HEAT-SQUELCHER PUNCH

1 quart boiling water
8 cranberry tea bags
1 large can (12 ounces)
  frozen apple juice
  concentrate, reconstituted
  according to can directions
½ lemon, sliced
1 orange, sliced
Crushed ice
Lemon balm sprigs
1 cup fresh strawberries,
  rinsed, hulled, and sliced

When Seattle's summer droughts leave you feeling wilted, reach for a glass of this jewel-toned punch. It's one of the most refreshing nonalcoholic drinks I have ever tasted.

——

In a large container, pour boiling water over teabags and let steep until tea is tepid, very strong, and bright red (about 45 minutes). Remove tea bags, squeezing out all liquid. Mix tea, apple juice, lemon slices, and orange slices. Refrigerate until cold or for up to 3 days. Transfer to a large insulated picnic jug. Pour into ice-filled glasses; garnish with lemon balm sprigs and sliced strawberries.

Makes about 2½ quarts (about 8 servings).

Beat the Heat Beach Barbecue for 8

Marinated Flank Steak Rolls with Pesto Filling ★
Melon Salad with Warm Blueberry Vinaigrette ★
Fresh Green Beans
Peasant Bread
White Burgundy Pie ★
St. Mary's Punch ★
Mineral Water
Beer
or
Dare to Run Naked ★

Fortunately, Northwesterners don't have to travel far to beat the heat: numerous beaches, many nearly in our backyards, dot the shores of Puget Sound and nearby lakes.

The dishes in this menu are easily started at home, requiring only finishing touches once you arrive at the beach.

For the salad, just toss chunks of your favorite melons with the warm vinaigrette on page 78.

MARINATED FLANK STEAK ROLLS
WITH PESTO FILLING

Pesto Filling (recipe follows)
2 pounds flank steak, fat
*   removed and meat scored*
¼ cup fresh lemon juice
¼ cup packed brown sugar
2 tablespoons Dijon mustard
2 tablespoons soy sauce
1 clove garlic, minced
¼ teaspoon freshly ground
*   black pepper*

These tender pinwheels of lean meat and aromatic pesto are quickly grilled. They taste great hot or cold—try one the next day in a sandwich (if you have any left, that is).

The meat must soak in its tangy-sweet marinade for at least 2 hours; if you like, you can marinate it en route to the picnic site.

———

Prepare Pesto Filling and refrigerate.

Place scored steak in a container with a lid. Mix remaining ingredients and pour over steak. Cover and refrigerate for at least 2 hours or up to 2 days. Transport steak in covered container to picnic site.

About 40 minutes before you are ready to eat, ignite coals and burn until white-hot. Remove meat from marinade, spread with Pesto Filling, and roll up tightly, securing with metal skewers. Cut crosswise into 8 (about 1-inch-thick) slices. Grill meat 3 inches from coals until done to your liking (about 5 minutes per side for medium).

Makes 8 servings.

PESTO FILLING
2 cups fresh basil leaves (1 ounce), rinsed, patted dry, and chopped
2 cloves garlic, minced
½ teaspoon salt
¼ to ½ cup pine nuts
½ cup olive oil
½ cup grated Asiago cheese

In a blender, combine basil, garlic, salt, and pine nuts; blend until puréed. With blender running, drizzle in oil in a slow, steady stream until entirely absorbed; then add cheese and blend until well mixed. Place in a small container, cover, and refrigerate until ready to transport to picnic or for up to 1 month.

Makes 1½ cups.

WHITE BURGUNDY PIE

5 eggs
1 tablespoon cold water
¾ cup sugar
⅛ teaspoon salt
½ cup white Burgundy
(Chardonnay)
9-inch pastry shell, baked
and cooled
3 ounces white chocolate,
grated
1 tablespoon unsalted butter

Swirls of white chocolate over a cloud-light, wine-flavored filling bring sophisticated elegance to your picnic.

————

Remove eggs from refrigerator and bring to room temperature; then separate. Place egg yolks and water in the top of a double boiler; beat until foamy. Whisk in sugar, salt, and wine. Then set over simmering water and beat with an electric mixer until thick and lemon-colored. Remove from heat; cool.

In a clean bowl, beat egg whites until stiff; fold into egg yolk–wine mixture and spoon into baked pastry shell.

Wash and dry top of double boiler; then melt chocolate with butter over simmering water, stirring until smooth. Swirl over pie. Refrigerate until chocolate is set and filling is firm (about 30 minutes).

Makes 8 servings.

St. Mary's Punch

2 oranges
2 lemons
2 limes
1 can (46 ounces) pineapple–
pink grapefruit juice,
chilled
Half of a 12-ounce can frozen
pink lemonade concentrate
1 quart 7-Up, chilled
3 tablespoons (1 jigger)
vodka per 1 cup punch
(optional)

Graduates of St. Mary's Hospital School of Nursing in Rochester, Minnesota, have been sharing this refreshing punch at their annual Seattle reunion for over 30 years. You may want to divide it between two jugs and add vodka to just one, providing a choice of alcoholic or nonalcoholic drinks. Either way, the punch will quench your guests' thirst and lower their temperature.

One day before the picnic, peel one *each* orange, lemon, and lime; then cut into small chunks. Fill 2 ice-cube trays with citrus chunks and water; freeze overnight.

The day of the picnic, thinly slice remaining orange, lemon, and lime. In a large insulated picnic jug, mix citrus slices, pineapple–pink grapefruit juice, and lemonade concentrate. At the picnic site, add 7-Up, and vodka if desired. Pour into glasses filled with the citrus-studded ice cubes.

Makes 8 servings.

Dare to Run Naked

About ½ cup (4 shots) gin
2 large cans (12 ounces
each) frozen lemonade
concentrate
2 bottles (22 to 24 ounces
each) beer, chilled
Crushed ice

Despite its strange ingredients, this drink is quite refreshing. If you're not careful, it may live up to its name and really loosen your inhibitions!

———

In a large thermos or insulated picnic jug, mix gin and lemonade concentrate and transport to picnic. Add beer at the last minute; pour into tall glasses filled with crushed ice.

Makes 8 servings.

AKA
Hop Step & Go Nakeds...

BELGIAN PICNIC FOR 15

Smoked Cheese Spread on Toast
Grilled Fresh Brisket
Crisp Endive with Pickled Beet Salad
Lemon Light Cheesecake ★
Belgian Chocolates
Tangerine-flavored Brandy
Strong Coffee
Beer

Belgians have long enjoyed fine food. Sixteenth-century Flemish paintings portray mouth-watering arrangements of vegetables and game, and modern city streets are lined with cafés, taverns, and elegant restaurants. The tempting window displays of the luxury food shops and the strong, pungent aroma of coffee from the brasseries proclaim a robust approach to life.

Tangerine-flavored brandy and superb chocolates are a favorite close to a Belgian meal. The luscious cheesecake in this menu also comes from a Belgian recipe.

LEMON LIGHT CHEESECAKE

4 eggs
1 cup cold water
½ cup sugar
1½ envelopes unflavored
  gelatin
½ cup water
4 packages (3 ounces each)
  cream cheese, softened
1½ tablespoons fresh lemon
  juice
1 cup graham cracker
  crumbs
¼ cup sugar
¼ cup butter, softened
1 cup whipping cream

At last, a light, mouth-watering cheesecake that will leave you feeling refreshed rather than heavy. Unlike the New York variety, Belgian cheesecakes are sublimely airy. I received the recipe in the early sixties from a grateful father after the birth of his daughter. Each time I prepare it, I relive the moment when I watched him count her fingers and toes.

––––––––

Remove eggs from refrigerator and bring to room temperature; then separate.

In the top of a double boiler, mix 1 cup cold water, ½ cup sugar, and gelatin. Set over simmering water and stir until gelatin is dissolved. In a small bowl, beat ½ cup water and egg yolks with an electric mixer until blended. Add to hot gelatin mixture; heat, stirring constantly, until thickened (about 8 minutes). Remove from heat.

In a large bowl, beat cream cheese and lemon juice until creamy. With a rubber spatula, blend in hot gelatin mixture until thoroughly combined. Refrigerate until thickened but not completely set (about 45 minutes).

Combine graham cracker crumbs, ¼ cup sugar, and butter. Press half the mixture into a buttered 9-by-13-inch pan.

In a chilled bowl, beat cream until stiff; fold into cheese mixture. Then, in a clean bowl, beat egg whites until stiff; fold into mixture. Pour over crust; top with remaining graham cracker crumb mixture. Refrigerate until firm (3 to 4 hours) or for up to 1 week.

Makes 15 servings.

FLORAL BASKET PARTY FOR 8

Pasta Prima-Orange *
Fruit and Floral Salad with Warm Blueberry Vinaigrette *
Mustard Bread Wedges
White Chocolate Mousse with Candied Rose Petals *

or

Lavender Sorbet
Indian Nut Cream *

or

Iced Rosehip Tea

Northwest restaurants, from Sooke Harbour House in British Columbia to Fall City Herb Farm east of Issaquah, have long used edible blossoms in their dishes. Mark Musick of Larry's Markets deserves much of the credit for spreading this colorful practice. After careful reading, I now know which blooms in my garden are safe and most flavorful.

I know rosehip tea is available in my favorite food shop but I enjoy growing my own. Although the petals of the *rosa rugosa* are lovely and edible, its rosehips, high in vitamin C, are the most valuable part of the bush. Pick the red-orange globes in the fall, then dice, and either dry or freeze the fruit for a healthful and tangy tea. Bring 1 tablespoonful in 1¼ cups of water to a boil and steep 15 minutes. Pour over ice.

PASTA PRIMA-ORANGE

3 tablespoons butter
2 shallots, minced
2 cloves garlic, minced
3 tablespoons all-purpose
flour
½ teaspoon salt
½ cup orange-flavored
liqueur
1 orange, peeled, sectioned,
and cut into chunks
1 tablespoon champagne
mustard
1 cup half-and-half
2 packages (about 10 ounces
each) fresh linguine

A dish at the Westin's Market Cafe inspired this rich, superb sauce for pasta. The gentle tang of fresh oranges beautifully accents the flavor.

———

In a wide frying pan, melt butter. Add shallots and garlic and sauté until browned. Stir in flour and salt. Add liqueur and stir until bubbly. Add orange pieces and mustard; heat through. Gradually add half-and-half; cook, stirring, until thickened. Remove from heat.

Following package directions, cook linguine; drain well. Pack pasta and sauce in separate covered containers. Wrap in newspapers and transport to picnic site. To serve, pour sauce over pasta and toss to mix.

Makes 8 servings.

FRUIT AND FLORAL SALAD WITH WARM BLUEBERRY VINAIGRETTE

1 cup fresh ripe blueberries, rinsed and drained

¼ cup olive oil

½ cup cubed fresh mozzarella cheese

Warm Blueberry Vinaigrette (recipe follows)

1 quart washed, crisped mixed salad greens, such as romaine lettuce, leaf lettuce, and watercress, torn into bite-size pieces

1 cup fresh edible blossoms or petals, such as violets, geraniums, nasturtiums, and rose petals

¼ cup toasted, skinned, chopped hazelnuts

When you make this salad, be sure to select blooms untouched by insecticides or pets; I avoid these problems by keeping pots of edible flowers on my deck.

The warm vinaigrette is so delicious you'll want to splash it on every salad you create from now on.

———

In a blender, purée ½ cup of the blueberries. Add oil. Place cheese cubes in a bowl; pour blueberry mixture over them and let stand while preparing vinaigrette.

Drain marinated cheese; place in a small container and cover tightly. Transport remaining ½ cup blueberries, greens, blossoms, and hazelnuts to picnic in separate covered containers.

At the picnic site, mix greens and blossoms in a large bowl. Add cheese; then toss mixture with a light coating of vinaigrette. Top with hazelnuts and remaining ½ cup blueberries, then serve.

Makes 8 servings.

WARM BLUEBERRY VINAIGRETTE
1 clove garlic, finely minced
2 tablespoons prepared sweet mustard
¼ cup white wine vinegar
1 teaspoon salt
10 grinds fresh black pepper
¼ cup fresh lemon juice
⅓ cup olive oil
⅓ cup walnut or vegetable oil
⅔ cup fresh blueberries, rinsed and drained
1 tablespoon sugar
3 tablespoons water

In a blender, combine first 6 ingredients. Blend until mixed. With blender running, gradually drizzle in oils in a slow, steady stream until entirely absorbed. Set aside.

In a small saucepan, heat blueberries, sugar, and water. When berries are softened, mash with a spoon and simmer for 1 minute. With blender running, slowly pour berry mixture into oil mixture. Transport to picnic site in a thermos.

Makes about 1 cup.

WHITE CHOCOLATE MOUSSE WITH CANDIED ROSE PETALS

4 eggs
¼ cup superfine sugar
2 tablespoons cognac
6 ounces white chocolate,
*   finely chopped*
3 tablespoons white crème
*   de cacao*
½ cup unsalted butter, cut
*   into ½-inch slices*
Candied Rose Petals (recipe
*   follows)*

Use only the finest Belgian chocolate for this recipe.

————

Bring eggs to room temperature; then separate. Place egg yolks and sugar in the top of a double boiler and beat with an electric mixer until thick and lemon-colored. Beat in cognac.

Set top of double boiler over simmering water and continue to beat until egg mixture is foamy and hot (about 4 minutes). Then set top of double boiler in a bowl of ice water and beat until mixture is cool and thick (about 4 more minutes).

In a heavy saucepan, melt chocolate with crème de cacao over low heat, stirring constantly. When chocolate is completely melted and smooth, beat in butter, one piece at a time, until mixture is smooth. Beat a small amount of the chocolate mixture into egg yolk mixture; then stir all egg yolk mixture into chocolate mixture.

In a clean bowl, beat egg whites until stiff. Stir a fourth of the whites into chocolate mixture; gently fold in remaining whites. Spoon into 8 individual dessert cups; refrigerate until set (about 4 hours). Top with Candied Rose Petals.

Makes 8 servings.

CANDIED ROSE PETALS
Freshly picked, dry roses (you will need 25 to 50 petals)
About ½ cup superfine sugar
1 egg white
1 teaspoon water

Edible flowers bring romance, color, and fragrance—the essence of a thriving garden—to your picnic. Whether the petals are tossed with salads or used to accent elegant desserts, they add a whimsical note to your menu.

The technique used here for rose petals works just as well for violets and other edible flowers. A list of edible flowers is available from The Herbfarm gift shop on Phinney Avenue North.

————

Pick roses away from the paths of neighborhood pets, choosing blooms that have not been spotted by water or sprayed with insecticides or fungicides. Select a flat pan large enough to dry petals in a single layer. Distribute a thin layer of sugar over bottom of pan.

In a small bowl, whisk egg white with water until frothy. Gently remove petals from roses and cut off white "heels." With a new, soft paintbrush, brush a thin layer of egg white mixture over both sides of each petal; using tweezers, gently dip each petal into sugar. Shake off excess so only one layer of sugar coats petal. Lay petals on sugared pan and let dry in the sun for 2 hours. To store petals, arrange carefully between layers of wax paper in tightly covered glass jars or tins. The candied petals will keep for up to 2 months.

Makes 25 to 50 candied petals.

INDIAN NUT CREAM

*¼ cup unsalted, unblanched
    pistachios*
*¼ cup unsalted, unblanched
    almonds*
¼ cup fresh rose petals
⅔ cup golden raisins
1 tablespoon anise seeds
*1 teaspoon freshly ground
    black pepper*
3 cardamom pods
¼ cup milk
1 quart milk
Rose water
Rose geraniums

This delicately flavored milk punch can be served as a beverage on its own, or used as a flavoring for brandy or rum punch.

Rosewater is sold in shops specializing in Far Eastern foods.

———

Place pistachios and almonds in a bowl and cover with cold water. Let stand overnight. Drain and remove skins. Place nuts in a blender with next 6 ingredients; blend for 30 seconds.

Place a clean cloth over a 1½-quart bowl. Pour nut mixture over cloth, being sure to scrape out any nut mixture remaining in blender. Slowly pour an additional quart of milk over nut mixture into bowl. Gather cloth around nut mixture; squeeze out all liquid. (Use solid nut remains in desserts or as a topping.)

Pour nut cream into a thermos; refrigerate until very cold (at least 24 hours). Serve chilled nut cream in small wineglasses to which a drop of rose water has been added; garnish with rose geranium blossoms.

Makes 8 servings.

Japanese Cooler for 5

Umeboshi (Pickled Plums)
Endamame (Green Soybeans in the Pod) *
Cold Somen (White Wheat Noodles) with Dipping Sauce *
Honeydew Melon Balls
Hawaiian Mochi *
Iced Green Tea
or
Hiyashi Mugicha (Iced Barley Tea) *
Kirin Beer

In Japan, more than in any other country, traditions and the foods served each month are dictated by the season.

The *umeboshi* listed in the menu are small, salty pickled apricots (called plums in Japan). They'll really make your mouth pucker — but during the hot, humid months on an island like Honshu, they are an essential source of the sodium lost through perspiration. In fact, the Japanese believe that one pickled plum a day will ensure a long and robust life. Many Japanese families pickle their own crocks of fruit, but in Seattle, you'll find umeboshi at Larry's Markets as well as in Asian markets.

Local Asian markets carry all the ingredients for the other items on this menu, as well.

ENDAMAME
(GREEN SOYBEANS IN THE POD)

The humble, healthful soybean is one of Japan's most popular summer pub snacks. Steamed in their pods, the beans are addictive and, when served with cold sake or a frosty mug of Kirin or Sapporo draft beer, quite refreshing. To eat them Japanese-style, just squeeze the pods and pop the delicious beans right into your mouth.

———

To prepare green soybeans (fresh or frozen), gently steam or boil the unshelled beans for 6 to 7 minutes. (Cooking the beans inactivates an enzyme, thus ensuring your body's absorption of the protein.) Then drain the beans, rinse them in cold water, drain again, and serve the pods in a large bowl, accompanied with beer or sake.

In Japan, endamame are sold and served still clinging to their stems. In the Northwest, they are available frozen in clear plastic bags in local Asian food stores.

COLD SOMEN WITH DIPPING SAUCE

Soba-jiru (Dipping Sauce),
recipe follows
2½ quarts water
2 bundles (5 to 8 ounces
each) somen
2 to 3 cups cold water
Ice water
Small green leaves
Condiments: Grated fresh
gingerroot, wasabi
(Japanese horseradish)
powder or paste, and
chopped fresh green shiso
(perilla), parsley,
cilantro, or watercress

Just the sight of these slender wheat noodles floating in bowls of ice water is refreshing. Japanese etiquette requires you to show your enjoyment by slurping each chopstickful noisily.

The noodles come in white, pink, green, and yellow; combining colors makes for a prettier dish.

———

Prepare sauce.

While sauce is chilling, cook the noodles. In a kettle, bring 2½ quarts water to a boil. Add somen and 1 cup of the cold water. Return to a boil. Add 1 more cup of the cold water. Return to a boil. Test noodles by dipping a strand in cold water; it should be translucent and pliable. If it is not, add 1 more cup of cold water and return to a boil.

Drain noodles and rinse under cold running water. Transport noodles and sauce to picnic site in separate covered containers. At the picnic site, place noodles in a large crystal bowl filled with ice water. Decorate with small green leaves. Pour sauce into 5 small crystal bowls; let picnickers add their choice of condiments to sauce, then dip each bite of noodles in sauce.

Makes 5 servings.

SOBA-JIRU
2 cups dashi (bonito stock)
5 tablespoons light soy sauce
3 tablespoons sugar
2 tablespoons mirin (sweet rice wine)
1½ tablespoons dark soy sauce

In a small saucepan, combine all ingredients. Cook over low heat, stirring constantly, until sugar is dissolved. Cool, then refrigerate until cold.

Makes about 2 cups.

Hawaiian Mochi

4 cups mochi flour (sweet
  glutinous rice flour)
1 tablespoon baking powder
½ cup butter, softened
3 cups sugar
4 eggs
1 can (12 ounces) coconut
  milk
1 can (12 ounces) evaporated
  low-fat milk
About 1 cup water
2 teaspoons vanilla
3 tablespoons sesame seeds,
  toasted

The Japanese who emigrated to Hawaii used island products to create a coconut custard version of a traditional confection. This recipe traveled from Hawaii to Okinawa, where my sister Ann first tasted it at a friend's home, then recrossed the Pacific with me to Seattle.

———

Preheat oven to 350°F. Butter a 9-by-13-inch baking pan and dust with flour.

Mix 4 cups mochi flour with baking powder. Set aside.

In a large bowl, cream butter and sugar with an electric mixer until light and fluffy. Add eggs, one at a time, beating well after each addition.

Pour coconut milk and evaporated milk into a large glass measure; add enough water to make 1 quart liquid total. With mixer running, gradually add milk-water mixture to creamed mixture alternately with dry ingredients.

Stir in vanilla. Pour batter into prepared pan, sprinkle with sesame seeds, and bake in preheated oven until a wooden pick or cake tester inserted in center of mochi comes out clean (about 1 hour). Cool, then cut into about 2-by-2½-inch pieces. Transport to picnic in a tightly covered container.

Makes about 2 dozen pieces.

HIYASHI MUGICHA

(ICED BARLEY TEA)

2 quarts water
2 cups mugi (roasted barley)
Crushed ice

Throughout Japan, barley tea is drunk to ease the oppression of the hot, muggy summers. Its slightly bitter flavor truly does revive one.

———

In a large saucepan, combine water and mugi and bring to a rapid boil over high heat. Reduce heat and simmer for 5 minutes. Remove pan from heat; cool tea to room temperature. Strain into an insulated picnic jug, discarding mugi. Refrigerate tea until very cold (at least 1 hour). To serve, pour into ice-filled glasses.

Makes 8 servings.

ICE CREAM SOCIAL FOR 10

Homemade Vanilla Ice Cream *
Cherry Sunshine *
Lace Gingersnaps
Todebeins *
Blondies (White Chocolate Brownies)
Old-fashioned Lemonade *

In the Midwest, ice cream socials are the perfect fund-raiser: everyone turns out for one scoop after another of smooth, rich homemade ice cream. The combinations my friends created depended on whether they favored butterscotch or chocolate topping, or black cows (root beer floats) or malteds. Arguments erupted over whether or not it was a sin to "spoil" a batch of pure vanilla ice cream by cranking fruit or maple syrup into it.

Between socials, my father took us out on hot summer nights for blue moon (blue ice cream) double-decker cones, root beer floats in frosted mugs, or thick, creamy milkshakes.

Each of the items on this menu, from the velvety ice cream to the tart, refreshing lemonade, is a traditional part of a Midwestern summer.

Homemade Vanilla Ice Cream

1 quart whole milk
3 eggs
2 cups sugar
4 teaspoons cornstarch
1 quart fresh raw whipping
  cream (available at local
  food co-ops)
1 tablespoon vanilla
About 2 cups chopped fresh
  fruit or nuts (optional)

During one of my last visits to my father, he spoke so vividly and fondly of this ice cream from his youth that I just had to track down the recipe. Thank heavens Mr. Berg, the son of the local pharmacist who used to make it, still had the recipe and was willing to share it with me. I think you will agree that this is the creamiest, most memorable vanilla ice cream you have ever tasted.

In the top of a large double boiler, bring milk almost to a boil over simmering water. Meanwhile, in a large bowl, beat eggs, sugar, and cornstarch with an electric mixer until well blended. Add to heated milk and continue to heat, stirring, until custard is thickened. Remove from heat and cool completely (about 1 hour). Add cream and vanilla and mix well. Pour into container of an electric ice-cream maker and refrigerate until next day.

Freeze ice cream according to manufacturer's directions; if desired, add fruit or nuts at this time. To store, pack into containers, cover tightly, and freeze for up to 1 month.

Makes 3 quarts (about 10 generous servings).

CHERRY SUNSHINE

4 cups sugar
1 quart fresh sour cherries,
  rinsed and pitted
½ cup light corn syrup

I have the warmest childhood memories of this topping spooned over vanilla ice cream. The recipe seems to preserve the essence of the fresh fruit, and makes a tangy foil for the sweet ice cream.

———

Preheat oven to 200°F. Spread sugar in a shallow baking pan and heat thoroughly. Place cherries in a deep kettle and gently mix in hot sugar by hand, being careful not to squash cherries. Cover kettle and place over very low heat until all sugar has melted; avoid scorching sugar. Carefully stir in corn syrup. Increase heat and bring mixture to boil. Boil for 5 minutes—no more—and remove from heat. Skim off bubbles and scum.

Carefully lift out cherries with a slotted spoon and line a shallow pan one layer deep. Cook syrupy juice in kettle for 10 more minutes, then pour over cherries. Cover pan with a pane of glass.

Set pan in full sun for 2 to 3 days, depending on thickness desired. Stir once or twice daily. Take pan in each evening at sunset.

Pour cherry mixture into a hot, sterilized jar (or jars); seal with 2 thin coats of paraffin, then add lids. Store for up to 3 months. Serve warm or cold over Homemade Vanilla Ice Cream.

Makes 2 cups (10 servings).

TODEBEINS

(DEAD MEN'S LEGS)

1 egg
½ cup sugar
⅓ cup finely chopped
blanched almonds
½ cup all-purpose flour

My great-grandmother, Barbara Forman Palen, brought the recipe for these light cookies (she called them *toad-a-bineys*) from Luxembourg. Despite their rather hair-raising name, the cookies are delicious—crisp, crunchy, and perfect with ice cream.

Preheat oven to 325°F. In a large bowl, beat egg lightly. Gradually add sugar and beat with an electric mixer until light and foamy (about 20 minutes). Add almonds and flour. Mix thoroughly. On a very lightly floured surface, roll dough into finger-thick ropes. Flatten slightly; cut into 3-inch lengths and arrange on ungreased baking sheets. Bake in preheated oven until lightly browned (about 10 minutes). Remove from baking sheets and cool completely on racks. Store airtight for up to 1 month.

Makes 2 dozen cookies.

OLD-FASHIONED LEMONADE

2½ cups sugar
2½ cups water
1¼ cups fresh lemon juice
2½ quarts water
20 lemon slices
Crushed ice
10 fresh lemon balm sprigs

There's no equal to lemonade made from fresh-squeezed lemons. You may, however, wish to reduce the amount of sugar in this recipe.

———

In a large saucepan, combine sugar and 2½ cups water. Heat, stirring constantly, until sugar is dissolved; then bring to a full rolling boil. Remove from heat. Cool. Add lemon juice and 2½ quarts water. If made in advance, cover and refrigerate for up to 3 days.

To serve, place a lemon slice in each of 10 tall glasses; fill glasses with crushed ice. Pour in lemonade. Adorn each glass with a lemon balm sprig and another lemon slice.

Makes 10 servings.

SEASHELLS BY THE SEASHORE FOR 6

Grilled Prawns in Mustard-Lime Marinade *
White Rice
Vegetable Bread
Cabbage Slaw
Frosted Wine Grapes with Cheese Wedges
Light Ale
Ice Water with Lemon Wedges

A simple yet elegant picnic. Everything but the main dish can be easily purchased at one of the area's superb take-out food shops. Just grab your hibachi and charcoal for the prawns, then head for a beach you've yet to try.

If you live on the east side of Lake Washington, head west to Lincoln Park, Gas Works Park, or Foster Island. If you live closer to Seattle, try Luther Burbank, Gene F. Coulon, or Newcastle Beach parks for a change of view.

GRILLED PRAWNS IN
MUSTARD-LIME MARINADE

¼ cup fresh lime juice and
   pulp
¼ cup extra-virgin olive oil
3 tablespoons Dijon mustard
1 tablespoon chopped fresh
   tarragon or rosemary
1 tablespoon snipped fresh
   chives
2 shallots, minced
4 large cloves garlic, minced
24 large prawns (31 to 40 per
   pound), shelled and
   deveined (leave tails
   intact)
4 cups cooked white rice

Serve hot over cooked white rice, smothered in the heated marinade. The tangy, herb-seasoned marinade can be prepared ahead of time; cook the rice at the last minute and wrap the pot in newspapers to transport to the picnic.

———

In a bowl, whisk lime juice and pulp with oil. Stir in mustard, tarragon or rosemary, chives, shallots, and garlic. Layer prawns with marinade in a glass dish. Cover and transport in a cooler to picnic site.

About 40 minutes before you are ready to eat, ignite coals and burn until white-hot. Drain prawns, reserving marinade. Grill prawns, 12 at a time, 3 inches from coals, until they are completely opaque (about 1 minute per side). At the same time, heat marinade in a small pan over side coals. As prawns are cooked, remove them from grill and keep warm in foil until all are cooked.

Makes 6 servings.

GARDEN LUNCHEON FOR 8

Hazelnut Leek Tart with Gruyère Cheese Pastry *
Shades of Green Salad
Fresh Orchard Fruit
Kir Royale *
Orange Lemonade *

Leeks have a long and noble history. Used in ancient Greek, Roman, and Egyptian preparations, they are known as "the asparagus of the poor" by the French. I first learned to enjoy their mild onion flavor when I discovered a cookbook devoted entirely to leek recipes in my local library. *The Leek Cookbook* was written by Mary Preus (Hamilton at the time), owner of the Silver Bay Herb Farm.

Herbs, spinach, cabbages, and lettuces come in a medley of greens, from dusky gray-green to bright yellow-green. You should have no trouble creating a multihued bowl of crisp, garden salad leaves.

HAZELNUT LEEK TART WITH GRUYÈRE CHEESE PASTRY

Gruyère Cheese Pastry Shell
  (recipe follows)
¼ cup nut or vegetable oil
2 medium leeks, trimmed,
  cleaned, and cut into thin
  slices (save some of tops to
  make leek bows)
2 cloves garlic, minced
1½ cups half-and-half
1 cup hazelnuts, chopped
2 teaspoons hot pepper sauce
½ teaspoon salt
3 eggs
1 cup grated Gruyère cheese
Leek bows

This is a cosmopolitan Northwest version of an old standby. It's tasty warm or cold, making it a most versatile picnic dish. Both filling and crust feature a generous helping of hazelnuts (toast and skin them before chopping, if you like).

———

Prepare and bake pastry shell. Reduce oven temperature to 350°F. Cool pastry shell completely while preparing filling.

To prepare filling, heat oil in a wide frying pan. Add leeks and garlic; sauté until golden brown. Remove from heat. Cool completely.

Remove pie weights and foil from pastry shell; spread leek mixture in bottom of shell. Protect edges of pastry shell from browning too quickly by covering with strips of foil.

Combine half-and-half, hazelnuts, hot pepper sauce, salt, and eggs in a blender; blend until smooth. Pour mixture over leeks, then sprinkle with cheese.

Bake in preheated oven until golden brown (about 35 minutes). Let stand for 10 minutes. Serve warm or cold, sliced into thin wedges and garnished with thin leek strips tied into double bows. If planning to serve warm, wrap in foil, then in newspapers, before transporting to picnic.

Makes 8 servings.

GRUYÈRE CHEESE PASTRY SHELL
1¼ cups all-purpose flour
½ teaspoon salt
⅛ teaspoon cayenne pepper
6 tablespoons cold unsalted butter
½ cup grated Gruyère cheese
½ cup finely chopped hazelnuts
4 to 5 tablespoons ice water

In a bowl, combine flour, salt, and cayenne. Cut in butter and cheese with a pastry cutter until mixture resembles coarse meal. Add hazelnuts. Sprinkle ice water evenly over flour mixture; stir with a fork until evenly moistened. Gather dough together, flatten, wrap in plastic wrap, and refrigerate for 30 minutes.

Preheat oven to 425°F. Roll out pastry ⅛-inch thick on a lightly floured marble slab or flat surface. Arrange in a buttered 11-inch tart pan. Trim edges, leaving a ½-inch overhang. Fold overhang under and flute. Line shell with wax paper, then fill with dried beans or aluminum pie weights. Bake in preheated oven until edges are lightly browned (about 20 minutes).

KIR ROYALE

*2 bottles (750 ml. each)
champagne, chilled*
About 1 cup crème de cassis

Crème de cassis, the famous black currant liqueur from Burgundy, adds an intriguing flavor to this cold drink.

Pour champagne into glasses; add 1 to 2 tablespoons crème de cassis to each serving.

Makes 8 servings.

ORANGE LEMONADE

6 lemons
1 can (12 ounces) frozen
   orange juice concentrate
1½ quarts water
1 cup sugar
1 tray (about 16) ice cubes
Crushed ice

Don't be tempted to mix this in the blender; it's better if you crush the lemon slices by hand.

———

Slice lemons and remove seeds. In a large insulated picnic jug, mix lemon slices, orange juice concentrate, water, sugar, and ice cubes. Mix thoroughly, mashing lemon slices as you stir. Refrigerate until very cold (at least 2 hours). At the picnic site, pour into glasses filled with crushed ice.

Makes 8 servings.

Victorian Lawn Party for 8

Cold Peach Soup with Gingered Crème Fraîche Topping *
Veal Terrine
Saffron Buns
Miniature Pecan Tarts *
Sunbrewed Tea
Berry Shrub *

Picture yourself and your guests on the grassy bank in Georges Seurat's painting, *A Sunday Afternoon on the Island of la Grande Jatte:* light filtering through willow trees, wicker baskets bursting with tempting fare, butterflies flitting from flower to flower. Choose the right spot, stretch out on your blanket, and while away the afternoon. Don't forget to bring a book of poetry—or better yet, compose your own.

To evoke the warmth of the summer sun, I have purposely chosen golden-colored dishes for this menu.

COLD PEACH SOUP WITH GINGERED CRÈME FRAÎCHE TOPPING

*1 quart peeled, sliced fresh
  peaches*
2 cups plain yogurt
1 cup half-and-half
½ cup packed brown sugar
*6 tablespoons peach schnapps
  or brandy*
1 teaspoon vanilla
1 teaspoon ground cinnamon
¼ teaspoon ground nutmeg
¼ fresh peach, peeled
¼ cup white wine vinegar
*½ cup Crème Fraîche (recipe
  follows)*
¼ teaspoon ground ginger
*Scented geraniums, fresh
  blueberries, or fresh
  raspberries*

A smooth, sweet soup that feels like cool velvet on your tongue.

———

In a blender, combine all ingredients except a quarter of the peach, vinegar, Crème Fraîche, ginger, and garnishes. Blend until smooth. Cover and refrigerate until cold (about 1 hour) or for up to 1 week. Transport to picnic site in a thermos or insulated picnic jug.

Before serving, in a small bowl, mash the peach quarter into vinegar; swirl into Crème Fraîche. Stir in ginger. Serve cold soup in small fancy glass bowls, topping each serving with a dollop of flavored Crème Fraîche. Add geranium blossoms or a few blueberries or raspberries as a final accent.

Makes 8 servings.

CRÈME FRAÎCHE
2 tablespoons plain yogurt or buttermilk
1 cup fresh whipping cream

Crème fraîche is used so extensively in French dishes that it's helpful to have a recipe for an easy substitute. Depending upon the dish, you may wish to lace the crème fraîche with Calvados or flavored vinegars, then use it as a topping for soups, fruit, or flans or mix it into drinks (see Spring Fever Cure, page 39, for example).

————

In an opaque crock, mix all ingredients thoroughly. Cover and let stand at room temperature until thickened (at least overnight). Then store in the refrigerator, covered, for up to 1 week.

Makes 1 cup.

MINIATURE PECAN TARTS

*2 packages (3 ounces each)
cream cheese, softened
1 cup butter, softened
1 cup all-purpose flour
2 eggs
⅛ teaspoon salt
2 tablespoons butter, melted
1½ cups packed brown sugar
1 teaspoon vanilla
1 cup pecan bits*

Watch these pastries disappear as soon as they come out of the oven.

———

In a large bowl, beat cream cheese and 1 cup butter until blended. Gradually add flour, beating until mixed; dough will be soft. Cover and refrigerate until firm.

Preheat oven to 350°F. In a medium bowl, beat eggs, salt, melted butter, sugar, and vanilla until blended.

Work with only small portions of the chilled dough at a time. Pinch off pieces of dough and form into walnut-size balls. Place each ball in a tiny muffin cup; press evenly against bottom and sides of cup with your thumb. Place a few bits of pecan in each cup, then spoon a small amount of filling over pecans.

Bake in preheated oven for 15 minutes, then reduce oven temperature to 250°F and continue to bake until filling is firm (about 10 more minutes).

Cool and remove from pans. If made in advance, package airtight and store for up to 1 week.

Makes 4 dozen tarts.

NOTE: Nonfat quark may be used in place of cream cheese.

BERRY SHRUB

*6 quarts hulled fresh
  strawberries or fresh
  raspberries, rinsed and
  drained*
1 quart berry vinegar
*2 cups sugar for each 2 cups
  juice*
Cold water or seltzer water

A favorite Victorian refresher, perfect for capturing the essence of that time.

———

Place 3 quarts of the berries in a large crock or glass jar; pour vinegar over berries. Let stand for 24 hours. Strain through a jelly bag or cheesecloth, pressing out all liquid. Pour liquid over remaining 3 quarts berries in crock or glass jar. Let stand for 24 more hours. Strain juice and measure it; then measure out 2 cups sugar for each 2 cups juice. In a large kettle, combine sugar and juice. Bring to a boil; boil for 20 minutes. Bottle in a sterilized 1-quart bottle. Cork.

For each serving, combine ⅛ cup berry concentrate with enough water or seltzer to fill one 8-ounce glass.

Makes 3 cups (enough for 24 servings).

WHITE LACE CREAM TEA FOR 10

Individual Salmon Mousses with Cucumber Sauce *
Chudleighs *
with
Fresh Strawberries and Clotted Cream *
White Eyelet Cutouts *
Peaches and Cream Punch *
or
Champagne
Tea with Lemon and Gingered Sugar

Fuss a little with this tea. Send invitations with lace borders and ask your guests to dress in white. Try to find a site with a gazebo (like the one at Meridian Park). Spread the ground or picnic table with a white lace tablecloth and napkins, then set it with all-white plates and teacups. Cover the teapot with a dainty white cozy.

For each guest, fashion a pure white tussie-mussie—a small, doily-wrapped bouquet in which each flower or herb is chosen to convey a specific sentiment. Silver Bay Herb Farm will make tussie-mussies to order for you; you can call the herb farm at (206) 692-1340 or drop by the stall at the Pike Place Market.

Finally, remember to capture the afternoon on film. Now wasn't it all worth it?

INDIVIDUAL SALMON MOUSSES
WITH CUCUMBER SAUCE

Vegetable oil
1¼ pounds salmon fillets,
   skinned and boned
¾ teaspoon salt
¼ teaspoon freshly ground
   black pepper
1 teaspoon Worcestershire
   sauce
1 teaspoon bottled onion juice
3 egg whites
1 cup whipping cream
Cucumber Sauce (recipe
   follows)

Airy bites of fresh salmon softly flavored with cucumber.

———

Preheat oven to 350°F. Oil a baking pan; place salmon in pan and bake in preheated oven until salmon is opaque throughout (about 4 minutes per side). Turn into a large bowl and mash evenly. Add salt, pepper, Worcestershire sauce, and onion juice; mix well. Add unbeaten egg whites, one at a time, blending well after each addition. In a chilled bowl, beat cream until stiff; fold into salmon mixture. Spoon into 10 oiled 1-cup fish-shaped molds. Cover and refrigerate until set (about 4 hours) or for up to 2 days. Meanwhile, prepare Cucumber Sauce.

At the picnic site, pour a few tablespoons of Cucumber Sauce onto each small serving plate; unmold an individual mousse atop each pool of sauce.

Makes 10 servings.

CUCUMBER SAUCE
½ cup mayonnaise, commercial or homemade
  (recipe on page 31)
2 tablespoons red wine vinegar
½ cup sour cream or plain nonfat yogurt
½ teaspoon bottled onion juice
½ teaspoon salt
1 cup peeled, seeded, chopped cucumber
1 tablespoon snipped fresh dill

In a bowl, combine ingredients in the order listed; mix well. Pour into a jar and refrigerate until ready to transport to picnic site.

Makes 2 cups.

CHUDLEIGHS

1 large egg, lightly beaten
About ¾ cup lukewarm water
(about 110°F)
2½ teaspoons active dry yeast
4½ cups all-purpose flour
2 tablespoons sugar
¼ teaspoon salt
½ cup sugar
¼ cup butter, softened

These buns, named after a village in Devonshire, can be dusted with powdered sugar and served warm, smothered with fresh strawberries and clotted cream.

———

Place egg in a 1-cup measure; add enough lukewarm water to fill. In a large bowl, mix yeast and 3 tablespoons of the egg liquid to make a paste. Add remaining egg liquid. Add 1 cup of the flour and 2 tablespoons sugar to liquid; mix until smooth. Cover and let rise in a warm place for about 30 minutes or until doubled in bulk.

Sift remaining 3½ cups flour with salt into a large bowl. Make a well in center of flour and add ½ cup sugar. Gradually pour in risen yeast mixture, stirring to dissolve sugar; then thoroughly mix to form a soft, sticky dough. Turn out onto a floured marble slab or flat surface; knead butter into dough until dough is smooth and silky. Shape into a ball, place in a buttered bowl, cover with a warm, damp towel, and let rise in a warm place until doubled in bulk (about 45 minutes).

Turn dough out onto a floured marble slab or flat surface. Punch down and shape into balls the size of plums. Cover with a warm, damp towel and let rest for 5 minutes. Flatten each ball into a 2-inch disk; fold disks in half. Place on greased baking sheets, cover, and let rise for 40 minutes. Meanwhile, preheat oven to 450°F. Bake buns in preheated oven until lightly browned (about 10 minutes). Wrap in foil to keep warm for transport to picnic site. If made in advance, cool; then wrap airtight and store for up to 2 days. Reheat, wrapped in foil, before leaving for the picnic.

Makes about 2 dozen buns.

CLOTTED CREAM

1 to 2 gallons fresh, raw, nonhomogenized Jersey or Guernsey milk

Anyone who has visited Devonshire will have fond memories of this topping for fresh strawberries and scones. It is the essential ingredient for a summer cream tea. My British pen-friend, Avril Benson, taught me the secret to success: find a source of raw milk, one rich in butterfat. A pure Jersey or Guernsey herd is essential. If you cannot find a dairy farm nearby, check a local co-op for raw milk. Pike Place Creamery also carries raw Guernsey milk. (Don't worry—the slow heating of the risen cream more than pasteurizes it.)

Place generous dollops of clotted cream on sliced fresh strawberries and just-baked Chudleighs or scones. It's also a rich, nutty-tasting replacement for butter in many of your recipes.

————

Pour milk into 1 or 2 large, shallow, flat-bottomed stainless steel pans. (I use my large stainless steel electric frying pan so that later, when heating the milk, I can easily maintain the milk temperature at or just below 180°F.) Set in a cool, protected place (not in the refrigerator) until the cream rises to the top (12 to 24 hours).

Without disturbing cream layer, carefully place pan over burners on the range and heat slowly for 4 hours. Maintain temperature of milk at or just below 180°F at all times. In other words, do not allow milk to scorch or boil. If the procedure is done properly, the cream will turn a pale golden yellow, tiny bubbles will appear at the pan edges, and a circle will rise on its leathery crust.

Carefully remove pan from heat, again being careful not to break up cream layer. Set in a cool, protected place for 12 to 24 hours (again, not in the refrigerator).

Use a brass or stainless steel skimmer to skim layer of cream into an airtight, opaque crock, allowing milk to flow back through into pan. (Use this skimmed milk later in recipes.)

Clotted cream will keep in the refrigerator for up to 2 weeks, in the freezer for up to 3 months. To ease spreadability, bring to room temperature before serving.

Makes about 1 cup (10 servings).

WHITE EYELET CUTOUTS

1 cup butter, softened
1½ cups sugar
2 eggs
1 teaspoon vanilla
4½ cups all-purpose flour
1 teaspoon baking soda
Royal Icing (recipe follows)

These lacy cutouts add an elegant dimension to your cream tea. Use a bit of eyelet lace as a guide to creating a lovely white icing design on each cookie.

———

In a large bowl, cream butter and sugar until light and fluffy. Add eggs and vanilla; beat until blended. Mix flour and baking soda; add to creamed mixture, a fourth at a time, beating well after each addition. Wrap dough in plastic wrap and refrigerate for 1 to 1½ hours (no longer, or dough will become too stiff to roll out).

Preheat oven to 350°F. Cut off enough dough to make one large cookie (about a fist-sized ball); keep remaining dough refrigerated. Roll out dough ¼-inch thick on a well-floured marble slab or flat surface. Cut out the design of your choice (for example, an angel, unicorn, heart, or doily) with a sharp knife or 6-inch cookie cutter. Place shaped dough on a baking sheet lined with baking parchment. Use small aspic, jelly, or candy cutters, or plastic straws, or knitting needles to punch out holes resembling eyelet lace.

Bake cookie in preheated oven until set but not browned at edges (8 to 10 minutes). Remove from oven and cool on baking sheet for 1 minute. Then remove from sheet along with paper and cool completely. Repeat to shape and bake remaining 9 cookies.

Prepare Royal Icing. Decorate edges of cutouts with icing piped from a pastry bag, using a No. 1, 2, or 3 tip. For a fancy finishing touch, loop a narrow white satin ribbon through a hole at the top of each cookie.

Makes 10 large cookies.

ROYAL ICING

White of 1 large egg, at room temperature
¼ teaspoon cream of tartar
1¼ cups powdered sugar

In a bowl, beat egg white and cream of tartar until stiff (7 to 8 minutes). Gently mix in powdered sugar. Keep covered with a damp cloth when not using.

PEACHES AND CREAM PUNCH

1¼ cups milk
½ cup half-and-half
¾ cup white rum
¼ cup white crème de cacao
¼ cup peach brandy
3 tablespoons plus 1 teaspoon
  powdered sugar
2 cups peeled, mashed fresh
  peaches or thawed frozen
  peaches
2 cups crushed ice

Luscious, thick, and creamy. Serve chilled, in small glasses.

———

In a blender, combine all ingredients except ice. Blend until well mixed. Add ice; blend well again. Pour into a large thermos and refrigerate until ready to leave for picnic. Pour into small glasses to serve.

Makes 10 servings.

MIDSUMMER-NIGHT'S MADNESS FOR 6

Titania Cherry Soup *
Oberon Pine Nut–stuffed Mushrooms *
Puck's Iced Crab Claws
Peaseblossom Salad with Raspberry Splash *
Mustardseed Breadsticks *
Ale, Mead, and Pear Brandy

or

Hot Mulled Cider

This Shakespearean medley begs you to celebrate the summer solstice (the night of June 20) in a wooded glen beneath a shadowed moon. Part of the celebration involves identifying the time when

> *Green is gold,*
> *Fire is wet,*
> *Future's told,*
> *Dragon's met.*

The answer to the riddle, of course, is Midsummer's Eve, when ancient pagan sun-worship joins medieval Christian belief. Titania, Oberon, Puck, Peaseblossom, and Mustardseed are, of course, characters in Shakespeare's comedy, *A Midsummer-Night's Dream.* The traditional rituals all take place around a bonfire, so choose an appropriate spot, such as the stone fireplaces at Lincoln Park .

TITANIA CHERRY SOUP

*1 quart fresh Bing cherries or
other dark sweet cherries,
rinsed, stems removed*

1½ quarts water

3 whole cloves

½ cinnamon stick

*2 tablespoons grated lemon
peel*

*1 package (3 ounces) cherry-
flavored gelatin*

1 cup sour cream

Fresh mint leaves

Lemon slices

A sweet, spicy flavor to start off the night's festivities.

———

In a large kettle, combine cherries, water, cloves, cinnamon stick, and lemon peel. Bring to a boil; then reduce heat, cover, and simmer for 40 minutes. Strain mixture through cheesecloth or a sieve into a large bowl. Press all juices from fruit and discard skins, pits, and spices. Return liquid to kettle. Mix gelatin into sour cream; stir gradually into strained cherry liquid. Heat gently, stirring to dissolve gelatin. Remove from heat; cool; then refrigerate for at least 30 minutes.

Transport to picnic site in a large thermos or insulated picnic jug. Serve cool, with mint leaves and lemon slices floating in each bowl.

Makes 6 servings.

OBERON PINE NUT-STUFFED MUSHROOMS

12 large mushrooms,
brushed, stems removed
½ cup pine nuts, chopped
¼ cup freshly grated
Parmesan cheese
¼ cup half-and-half
½ teaspoon salt
¼ teaspoon hot pepper sauce
1 cup Italian-seasoned fine
dry bread crumbs

Bitefuls of the piny woods.

———

Hollow out mushroom caps, if necessary. In a medium saucepan, combine remaining ingredients. Heat over low heat, stirring until blended. Fill caps. Wrap in foil and transport to picnic site. At picnic site, heat wrapped mushrooms on a grill until hot throughout (about 15 minutes).

Makes 6 servings.

PEASEBLOSSOM SALAD
WITH RASPBERRY SPLASH

*Raspberry Splash (recipe
    follows)*
*½ cup each fresh black,
    golden, and red raspberries*
*½ cup seedless green grapes,
    rinsed and cut in half*
1 pear, cored and julienned
*1 quart washed, crisped mixed
    salad greens, torn into
    bite-size pieces*
*¼ cup grated white Cheddar
    cheese*
*3 tablespoons sesame seeds,
    toasted*
1 bunch pea tendrils
*1 cup snow or sugar snap
    peas, rinsed, drained, and
    destringed*

A crisp green salad layered with
wonderful surprises.

————

Prepare Raspberry Splash. In a
jar, cover raspberries, grapes, and
pear with Raspberry Splash.

Transport remaining prepared
salad ingredients in separate
covered containers to picnic site.

At picnic site, place greens in a
salad bowl. Add cheese, sesame
seeds, pea tendrils, and snow peas.
Drain fruit, reserving Raspberry
Splash; add fruit to salad. Sprinkle
salad lightly with reserved Raspberry Splash. Toss and serve.

Makes 6 servings.

RASPBERRY SPLASH

½ cup olive oil

¼ cup raspberry vinegar

½ teaspoon salt

¼ teaspoon freshly ground pink, white, black, or green peppercorns

1 tablespoon Crème Fraîche (recipe on page 103)

Northwest sunshine and berries captured in a bottle, then released on your salad.

In a cruet or screw-top jar, combine all ingredients and shake well. Refrigerate for at least 1 hour before using.

Makes ¾ cup.

MUSTARDSEED BREADSTICKS

¼ cup butter, softened
1 teaspoon Dijon mustard
½ teaspoon yellow mustard
  seeds, cracked
2 scallions, minced
1 teaspoon honey
1 package (11 ounces)
  refrigerated breadstick
  dough

Soft breadsticks glistening with a honey-mustard glaze.

———

Preheat oven to 350°F. In a bowl, beat together butter, mustard, mustard seeds, scallions, and honey. Set aside.

Bake twisted breadsticks on ungreased baking sheets for 6 minutes. Brush breadsticks with butter mixture and bake another 1 to 2 minutes, or until golden brown. Wrap in foil to transport to picnic site.

Makes 6 servings.

FALL POTLATCH FOR 12

Pink Marbled Eggs Stuffed with Deviled Crab *
Chicken Salad with Warm Toasted Seed Dressing *
Italian Sun-kissed Peasant Bread
with
Herbed Goat Cheese Butter *
Plum Cake
Wine
Seltzer Water

Gather your friends together around a warm fire to carry on the Northwest potlatch tradition of sharing the season's bounty. Each of these dishes can be made ahead of time.

Chances are you have a friend or neighbor who would love to share her overabundance of plums each fall. I look for Shiro (a hardy, delicious yellow variety), Damson, and Green Gage, but I'll take any that are ripe and ready for cake or chutney.

The Northwest has been fortunate in the increasing number of small, quality dairies and cheesemakers that supply local groceries. The many choices of fine goat cheese are one of the results. Combining mild chèvre with herbs and butter is a good way to introduce goat cheese to your guests.

Pink Marbled Eggs
Stuffed with Deviled Crab

6 eggs

Beet juice or other natural plant dye, such as red onion skins, spinach (for green eggs), or turmeric (for golden eggs)

2 tablespoons mayonnaise, commercial or homemade (recipe on page 31)

1 teaspoon champagne vinegar

½ teaspoon salt

Dash of white pepper

½ teaspoon prepared yellow mustard

½ cup shredded fresh crabmeat

These look elegant, but they are easy to make.

———

Place eggs in a saucepan, cover with cold water, and bring to a rapid boil. Reduce heat, cover, and simmer for 15 minutes. Rinse immediately in cold water. Roll eggs on a counter to crack shells, but do not remove shells. Soak eggs in beet juice for 30 minutes. Remove shells, cut eggs in half, and carefully remove yolks.

In a bowl, mash yolks with remaining ingredients, except crabmeat; then add crabmeat. Stuff eggs with filling. Cover and refrigerate until picnic time.

Makes 12 servings.

CHICKEN SALAD WITH WARM TOASTED SEED DRESSING

2 whole chicken breasts, split
4 chicken thighs
4 quarts washed, crisped
mixed salad greens, torn
into bite-size pieces
1 cup minced fresh lemon
balm
1 large firm-ripe avocado,
pitted, peeled, and sliced
2 large grapefruits, peeled,
sectioned, and cut into
chunks
1 cup julienned celery
⅓ cup julienned scallions
Toasted Seed Dressing
(recipe follows)
½ cup pine nuts, toasted

Toss the salad with the warm, aromatic dressing at the last minute—then stand back and watch it disappear.

———

The day before the picnic, bake chicken. Preheat oven to 350°F; arrange chicken pieces, skin side up, in a baking pan and bake in preheated oven, uncovered, until meat near bone is no longer pink (about 30 minutes). Cool chicken; discard skin and bones, then shred meat. Refrigerate.

The day of the picnic, prepare greens and lemon balm. Mix sliced avocado with grapefruit; add celery and scallions. Prepare dressing.

Transport chicken, greens, lemon balm, avocado mixture, and pine nuts to picnic site in separate containers. At picnic site, combine all salad ingredients in a large bowl. Toss warm dressing with salad; then add pine nuts.

Makes 12 servings.

TOASTED SEED DRESSING
⅓ cup nut or vegetable oil
3 tablespoons sesame seeds
½ teaspoon grated lemon peel
¼ cup fresh lemon juice
½ teaspoon dry mustard
1 tablespoon sugar
1 tablespoon soy sauce
Salt to taste

In a wide frying pan, heat oil over low heat. Add sesame seeds and toast, stirring often, until golden. Add remaining ingredients. Pour into a small thermos to transport to picnic site.

ITALIAN SUN-KISSED PEASANT BREAD
WITH HERBED GOAT CHEESE BUTTER

2 envelopes active dry yeast
3½ cups lukewarm water
(about 110°F)
2 teaspoons salt
10 cups bread flour
2 ounces prosciutto, diced
¼ cup sun-dried tomatoes, diced
About ¼ cup pitted green olives, chopped
Olive oil
Herbed Goat Cheese Butter (recipe follows)

Flavorful surprises kneaded into the dough make this bread distinctive as well as delicious. Serve it warm, with Herbed Goat Cheese Butter.

———

In a large bowl, dissolve yeast in lukewarm water and let stand for 5 minutes. Mix in salt, 5 cups of the flour, prosciutto, tomatoes, and olives; beat vigorously, adding enough of the remaining flour to make a smooth but not sticky dough.

Turn dough out onto a floured marble slab or flat surface. Knead, adding remaining flour as necessary, until dough is firm and elastic (about 10 minutes).

Place dough in a lightly oiled bowl. Cover with a warm, damp towel and let rise in a warm place until doubled in bulk (about 1 hour). Punch down.

Preheat oven to 350°F. Place dough on a large baking sheet brushed with oil; shape into a large circle. Make a hole in center of loaf and place an oiled small oven-proof bowl in center. Cover with a warm, damp towel and let rise until doubled in bulk (about 20 minutes). Bake in preheated oven until loaf is browned and sounds hollow when tapped (about 1 hour). Wrap in foil to keep warm until picnic. If made in advance, cool, wrap airtight, and store for up to 2 days. Reheat, wrapped in foil, before leaving for picnic. Serve with Herbed Goat Cheese Butter.

Makes 12 servings.

HERBED GOAT CHEESE BUTTER
¼ pound mild goat cheese (chèvre)
1 package (3 ounces) cream cheese, softened
¾ cup unsalted butter, softened
Salt and white pepper to taste
2 tablespoons snipped fresh chives
1 tablespoon minced fresh basil
2 tablespoons diced sun-dried tomatoes

A tasty country spread that perfectly enhances the steamy-hot peasant bread.

In a bowl, combine all ingredients and beat well with an electric mixer. Place in a crock that will fit in center of bread ring. Cover and refrigerate until picnic time. To serve, bring cheese spread to room temperature; place bread ring on a breadboard and center with cheese spread.

Makes 1 cup (12 servings).

FOOTBALL FEVER FEED FOR 4

Beer Cheese Soup in Cheese Pastry Bowls *
Meat on a Stick
Raw Vegetables and Crisp Apples
B.C. Chocolate Bars *
Beer and Wine
Coffee

Your favorite team is playing. Your guests are also ardent fans. What else do you need to enjoy a crisp fall afternoon? Plenty of wholesome food, of course. This menu gives you all the warmth and energy you'll need to cheer your men on from the 50-yard line. The meal can be dished up from your tailgate or served at a picnic spot near the stadium—on the University of Washington campus, in the Arboretum, or at the Center for Urban Horticulture, for example.

For the Meat on a Stick, be creative and make one or more kinds of shish kabob—use spicy meatballs, barbecued pork, steak cubes, or chicken chunks with apricot glaze.

BEER CHEESE SOUP
IN CHEESE PASTRY BOWLS

Cheese Pastry Bowls (recipe
follows)
3 cups chicken broth
¾ cup finely chopped shallots
½ cup finely chopped carrot
½ cup finely chopped celery
⅓ cup chopped green bell
pepper
¼ cup butter
¼ cup all-purpose flour
1 cup light ale
4 cups grated, firmly packed
sharp Cheddar cheese
1 teaspoon Dijon mustard
⅛ teaspoon cayenne pepper
¼ to ⅓ cup whipping cream
Salt to taste
Snipped fresh dill and
croutons; or Crème
Fraîche (recipe on page
103)

This tangy soup warms your insides all the way down. After the soup is gone, bite into the crisp pastry bowls.

———

Prepare Cheese Pastry Bowls.

In a saucepan, slowly heat broth while chopping shallots, carrot, celery, and bell pepper. In a large saucepan, melt butter; add vegetables and sauté until soft (about 10 minutes). Stir in flour and cook, stirring, for a few more minutes. Add heated broth and ale, a little at a time. Bring to a gentle boil, stirring frequently; then partially cover and simmer for 30 minutes. Strain mixture, discarding vegetables.

Return strained broth to saucepan. Slowly stir in cheese; continue to stir until completely melted. Add mustard, cayenne, and cream. Season to taste with salt.

Pour into a large thermos for transport to picnic site. Stir again

before serving in Cheese Pastry Bowls. Garnish with dill and croutons, or pipe Crème Fraîche designs on top.

Makes 4 servings.

CHEESE PASTRY BOWLS
2 cups all-purpose flour
¼ teaspoon salt
½ cup cold unsalted butter
½ cup grated white Cheddar cheese
Dash of cayenne pepper
1 tablespoon Dijon mustard
6 tablespoons ice water

In a bowl, combine flour and salt. Cut in butter with a pastry cutter
until mixture resembles coarse meal. Add cheese, cayenne, and
mustard. Blend by hand. Gradually add ice water, 1 tablespoon at a
time, until a stiff dough forms. Mold into a flattened oval, wrap in
plastic wrap, and refrigerate for 1 hour.

Preheat oven to 350°F. Butter outsides of 4 small (about 5-inch-
diameter) oven-proof bowls; set aside. Divide dough into 4 sections;
work with one at a time, leaving others in refrigerator. To shape
each bowl, roll out dough ¼-inch thick on a lightly floured marble
slab or flat surface. Drape rolled-out dough over inverted buttered
oven-proof bowl; gently press dough against bowl. Trim edges.

Place bowls on a baking sheet and bake in preheated oven until
golden brown (about 30 minutes). Carefully loosen pastry from
bowls, but to keep pastry from breaking, do not remove pastry from
bowls until you arrive at picnic site.

B.C. Chocolate Bars

½ cup butter
5 tablespoons unsweetened
cocoa powder
¼ cup sugar
1 egg, lightly beaten
2 cups graham cracker
crumbs
1 cup unsweetened shredded
coconut
½ cup chopped black walnuts
1 teaspoon vanilla
2 cups powdered sugar
3 tablespoons milk
¼ cup butter, softened
2 tablespoons Bird's English
custard powder
3 ounces (3 squares)
semisweet chocolate
1 tablespoon butter

By now, it seems that everyone in the Northwest must have the recipe for these chocolate bars from Nanaimo, British Columbia, but I recently met a few people who were amazed and delighted to taste them for the first time. My rendition of the recipe was inspired by Mrs. Florence Bibby's version, which she shared with my sister Carolyn in the early seventies.

Cut the rich bars into tiny pieces so you and your guests won't feel too guilty on the way home.

Bird's English custard powder is available at several local markets, including Larry's Markets.

Butter an 8-inch-square baking pan. In a saucepan, combine ½ cup butter, cocoa, and sugar. Place over low heat; stir until butter is melted. Add egg and cook, stirring, until mixture is thickened. Combine graham cracker crumbs, coconut, and walnuts. Add to cocoa mixture along with vanilla. Press into prepared pan.

Mix powdered sugar, milk, ¼ cup butter, and custard powder. Spread on top of crumb mixture and refrigerate for 30 minutes.

In a small saucepan, combine semisweet chocolate with 1 tablespoon butter. Melt over low heat, stirring constantly. Spread on top of chilled bars; refrigerate until topping is firm (about 30 minutes). These are rich, so cut into bite-size (about 1-inch-square) pieces. Covered tightly, the bars will keep for up to 1 month.

Makes 64 bars.

Gathering in the Wild for 6

Mushrooms in Filo Pastry *
Wilted Wild Greens
Black Walnut Crescents
Rhubarb Wine
Elderblossom Fizz *

The Northwest is renowned for wild edibles, especially for its wide variety of mushrooms. Certain species, such as the matsutake, are highly valued as gifts in Japan.

Just as valuable to me are jars of shelled black walnuts. When I was a young girl, our family made an annual fall excursion to gather these aromatic nuts, as well as bittersweet, hickory nuts, and butternuts. I remember my mother's stained hands as she dried and husked the black walnuts, then cracked the stone-hard shells with a hammer and picked out the kernels.

There are a few black walnut trees around the south end of Green Lake and on the University of Washington campus. Spend a day gathering walnuts and wild mushrooms and greens, then convert your bounty into a picnic.

For the Wilted Wild Greens, use your favorite hot bacon dressing on the greens you've collected. To make the cookies, just substitute black walnuts for the toasted almonds in the Almond Crescent recipe on page 181.

MUSHROOMS IN FILO PASTRY

2 tablespoons butter

3 tablespoons finely chopped scallions

½ pound mushrooms (such as shiitakes, matsutakes, chanterelles, or oyster mushrooms), brushed and chopped

3 tablespoons all-purpose flour

½ cup half-and-half

½ teaspoon salt

⅛ teaspoon cayenne pepper

1 tablespoon chopped parsley

½ teaspoon fresh lemon juice

2 tablespoons grated Parmesan cheese

3 sheets filo pastry, thawed if frozen

3 tablespoons cold butter

I first tasted these crisp pockets filled with mushrooms in the sun-filled kitchen of one of Seattle's best cooks, Carol Lindcroft. She, too, gathers recipes during her travels and brings them home to share.

————

In a wide frying pan, melt 2 tablespoons butter. Add scallions and sauté until soft. Add mushrooms and cook until liquid has evaporated. Remove from heat. Sprinkle mushroom mixture with flour; stir to blend, then stir in half-and-half. Return to heat and bring to a boil. Reduce heat and simmer, uncovered, until thickened. Remove from heat. Add salt, cayenne, parsley, lemon juice, and cheese. Mix thoroughly. Cool.

Preheat oven to 350°F. Butter a baking sheet. Place one filo sheet on a flat surface; dot with 1 tablespoon cold butter. Repeat with remaining filo sheets, layering successively. Cut stacked filo into six 6-inch squares; filo trimmings can be used to decorate final triangles. Place a sixth of the mushroom mixture in center of each square; fold over each square to form a triangle and press edges to seal. Place on prepared baking sheet. Bake in preheated oven until crisp and golden brown (about 30 minutes). Wrap in foil and transport to picnic site. If desired, recrisp pockets at picnic site: open up foil, place pockets on grill, and heat briefly.

Makes 6 servings.

NOTE: In place of half-and-half, you may use ½ cup nonfat buttermilk mixed with ½ teaspoon cornstarch.

ELDERBLOSSOM FIZZ

2 lemons
6 elderblossom flower heads
1½ pounds (about 3½ cups)
sugar
1 gallon cold water
2 tablespoons white wine
vinegar

The Blue Elderberry (*Sambucus cerulea*, formerly named *Sambucus glauca*) is a cousin of the shrub found in European hedgerows and is available in local nurseries and gardens. It also grows wild near the edges of fields and woods, where you'll find 8-inch flat, creamy-white blossom clusters (known as Elder Blow) blooming from April to August. If you make note of the bush's location when the blossoms are visible, you'll more easily find it in August or September when you return to gather the blue-black berries for drying or for making the much-prized jams, jellies, pies, or wine. By gathering the blue elderberry blossoms and fruit, you'll be carrying on an important Northwest Native American tradition. Fragrant, refreshing, and fizzy, this sweet drink is almost like champagne. You'll need to prepare it at least 2 weeks before your picnic.

———

Squeeze juice from lemons and set aside. Then cut juiced lemons into quarters; set aside. In a large bowl, combine blossoms, sugar, water, and vinegar. Drizzle with lemon juice. Add lemon quarters. Let mixture stand for 24 hours, stirring occasionally. Strain through a large sieve and bottle in 4 sterilized 1-quart bottles. Cork. Lay bottles on their sides and let rest for 2 weeks before serving. Elderblossom Fizz will keep for up to 6 months.

Makes 1 gallon.

Sister Cities' Celebration for 12

Bergen Pickled Salmon *
Kōbe Kasu Grilled Fish *
or
Lamb on a Spit
Tashkent Finger Salads (Stuffed Grape Leaves)
Nantes Beignets *
Guinness Extra Stout
Wine
Ginger-Juice Sparkler *

Celebrating the close friendship Seattle enjoys with each of her 16 sister cities is the perfect excuse for a picnic. As your guests enjoy the meal, you might hold an informal contest to see how many "sisters" each person can name. Besides the four cities listed in the menu above, they are: Dawson, Yukon Territory; Beer Sheva, Israel; Christchurch, New Zealand; Mazatlán, Mexico; Mombasa, Kenya; Chongqing, China; Limbe, Cameroon; Managua, Nicaragua; Galway, Ireland; Reykjavik, Iceland; Taejon, Korea; and Kaohsiung, Taiwan.

I'm afraid I'm guilty of using poetic license in naming these recipes!

BERGEN PICKLED SALMON

*1 pound salmon fillets,
skinned and boned*
3½ tablespoons salt
1 cup white vinegar
*2 tablespoons packed dark
brown sugar*
1 cup water
*1 teaspoon black mustard
seeds*
*1 teaspoon white mustard
seeds*
1 tablespoon pickling spices
*¼ teaspoon dried hot pepper
flakes*
*1 tablespoon dried juniper
berries*
*1 tablespoon each whole
pink, green, and black
peppercorns*
*1 medium white onion, thinly
sliced*

Served on toasts or rusks, pickled salmon is a wonderful opener to a picnic.

———

Rinse salmon, pat dry, and cut crosswise into ¼-inch slices. Sprinkle 1½ tablespoons of the salt over bottom of a 9-by-13-inch glass dish. Spread salmon pieces over salt. Sprinkle with remaining 2 tablespoons salt. Cover and refrigerate overnight.

In a small saucepan, bring vinegar, sugar, and water to boil. Remove from heat; cool. Rinse salt from salmon and pat dry. Mix black and white mustard seeds, pickling spices, hot pepper flakes, juniper berries, and peppercorns. In a 1-quart wide-mouth glass jar, alternate layers of salmon, onion slices, and mixed spices. Pour cooled vinegar mixture over layers. Screw on jar lid; refrigerate for at least 24 hours or for up to 1 month.

Makes 12 servings.

KŌBE KASU GRILLED FISH

¾ cup sake, warmed
1 cup sake kasu
¾ cup sweet white miso
3 tablespoons soy sauce
¾ cup plum wine
12 fresh fish fillets such as
   black cod or halibut (each
   1½ inches thick)
3 tablespoons olive oil

Here's your opportunity to follow a recent trend and share in the success of a few innovative Seattle restaurants and markets: marinate your fish in kasu—the dregs of sake production—before grilling it. Mixed with sake to form a paste, kasu imparts a glorious flavor to fish or vegetables.

Sake kasu resembles wet sand; it can be found in the fresh fish sections of Asian markets.

———

In a blender, combine all ingredients except fish and oil; blend until a thin paste forms. Spread a third of the paste over bottom of a glass dish; arrange fish on top. Cover with remaining paste. Cover and refrigerate for at least 4 hours or up to 24 hours.

About 40 minutes before you are ready to eat, ignite coals and burn until white-hot. Remove fish from paste. Pat dry. Brush fish with oil. Grill 3 inches from coals just until fish is opaque throughout (3 to 4 minutes per side); on each side, rotate fish 90 degrees halfway during cooking to create a crosshatch design.

Makes 12 servings.

NANTES BEIGNETS

1 envelope active dry yeast
½ cup lukewarm milk (about 110°F)
2 eggs, beaten
1½ teaspoons vanilla sugar
1½ cups butter, melted
½ teaspoon salt
1 teaspoon grated lemon peel
1½ tablespoons fresh lemon juice
1 teaspoon almond extract
½ cup evaporated low-fat milk
4 cups sifted bread flour
Canola (rapeseed) oil
Powdered sugar

These buttery puffs (pronounced ben-YEAH) are delightful for breakfast as well as dessert.

In a large bowl, dissolve yeast in ½ cup lukewarm milk and let stand for 5 minutes. Add eggs, vanilla sugar, butter, salt, lemon peel, lemon juice, almond extract, and evaporated milk. Gradually blend in flour, mixing well. Place in oiled bowl; cover. Refrigerate at least overnight or for up to several days.

Punch down dough; turn out onto a lightly floured marble slab or flat surface. Roll out ⅛-inch thick. Cut into 2½-inch squares. Cover with a warm, damp towel; let rest for 10 to 12 minutes. Meanwhile, in a deep, heavy frying pan, heat 2 inches of oil to 370°F.

Add beignets to oil; do not crowd pan. Cook, turning once and basting continually with oil, until beignets are puffy and golden brown (about 5 minutes). Remove with a slotted metal spoon and drain on paper towels. Toss in a paper bag with powdered sugar. Repeat until all beignets are cooked. Transport to picnic in an airtight container.

Makes 2 dozen beignets.

NOTE: Once found on every home baker's pantry shelf, vanilla sugar is simply granulated sugar (say, 4 cups) poured over (and flavored by) a split whole vanilla bean in a quart-sized covered jar or canister. The vanilla bean can be used in this way for up to one year without losing its potency. Simply keep refilling the jar with sugar, which absorbs the pleasant flavor of the bean and is used in baking or to sprinkle on toast, desserts, or waffles.

Vanilla sugar is stronger and sweeter than plain sugar, so use with caution. When a recipe calls for 1 cup or more, use ½ vanilla sugar and ½ plain sugar. Escoffier uses much less vanilla sugar than sugar in sweetened whipped cream and chocolate sauce recipes.

Local markets sell a product that is called Cook's Pure Vanilla Powder that is dextrose (sugar) flavored with vanilla beans.

GINGER-JUICE SPARKLER

*1 can (12 ounces) frozen
    grape juice concentrate
1 can (12 ounces) frozen
    orange juice concentrate
1 can (12 ounces) frozen
    lemonade concentrate
1 quart water
1 quart ginger ale, chilled
Crushed ice*

This is wonderfully refreshing.

———

In a 1-gallon insulated picnic jug, combine all ingredients except ginger ale and ice; stir well. Refrigerate for 2 hours. At the picnic site, add ginger ale and stir. Pour into ice-filled glasses.

Makes 12 servings.

Harvest Moon Watch for 12

Portuguese Red Bean Soup *
in
Pumpkin Bowls
Citrus Salad with Lime Dressing
Golden Herbed Pretzel Knots *
Apple Cake with Hot Rum Sauce *
Stout
or
Hot Cider

The vivid autumn colors and spicy aromas of these dishes invite your guests to draw closer and sample the tang and bounty of a Northwest harvest. Chunks of homemade sausage and golden pumpkin float in a layer of spices, herbs, and red beans atop a substantial rust-colored broth. The baby pumpkin bowls can also be a part of the feast. Simply steam them first to create an edible serving dish.

To make the salad, prepare a lime dressing using fresh lime juice, a little olive oil, plain yogurt, and seasonings; drizzle it over peeled fresh grapefruit and mandarin orange slices.

PORTUGUESE RED BEAN SOUP

*2 cups dried red kidney beans
or 2 large cans (28 ounces
each) red kidney beans
2 quarts water (2½ quarts if
using dried beans)
3 smoked ham shanks (about
1 pound each)
3 potatoes, peeled and diced
1 cup chopped carrots
¾ to 1 pound pumpkin or winter
squash (about half of a
small pumpkin or squash),
peeled, seeded, and diced
2 cans (8 ounces each)
tomato sauce
1 teaspoon ground allspice
2 bay leaves
1 teaspoon ground cumin
1 teaspoon ground cinnamon
2 tablespoons olive oil
1 medium onion, sliced
2 cloves garlic, minced
3 tablespoons chopped fresh mint
1 medium (8-inch-long)
Linguica (Portuguese
Sausage), recipe follows
1 bunch watercress, chopped
Salt and pepper to taste*

This rich, spicy soup will forever evoke the magic of Maui for me, where my life-long friend, Kathleen Rose Johnson, prepared it for our families one tropical Christmas.

Use hollowed-out miniature pumpkins as soup bowls; serve with Golden Herbed Pretzel Knots and hot cider or frosty mugs of stout. (If you plan to make your own linguica sausage, be sure to do so 1 to 3 days ahead of time.)

———

Use a 5-quart soup kettle. If using dried beans, cover with 1 quart of the water and bring to a boil; boil for 2 minutes, then remove from heat. Let stand for 1 hour. Add remaining 1½ quarts water. If using canned beans, simply fill kettle with 2 quarts water (and add beans later, as noted in following text).

Add ham shanks to kettle. Bring to a boil; then reduce heat, cover, and simmer until dried beans and meat are tender (about 45 minutes). Add canned beans (if using), potatoes, carrots, pumpkin or squash, tomato sauce, allspice, bay leaves, cumin, and cinnamon.

In a saucepan, heat oil; add onion, garlic, and mint. Sauté until onion is tender. Add to soup. In another saucepan, heat sausage, covered, in a small amount of water for 8 to 10 minutes. Cut up and add to soup. Add watercress. Simmer soup for 30 more minutes, then season to taste with salt and pepper. Remove bay leaves and ham shanks from soup; cut meat from ham shanks and add to soup. If made in advance, cool; cover and refrigerate for up to 1 week. Reheat before picnic.

Transport soup to picnic in a 1-gallon wide-mouth insulated picnic container with handles. To serve, ladle into small hollowed-out pumpkins or large mugs.

Makes 12 servings.

LINGUICA (PORTUGUESE SAUSAGE)
1½ teaspoons salt
¼ teaspoon freshly ground black pepper
2 teaspoons sweet paprika
1 teaspoon minced fresh rosemary
2 cloves garlic, minced
1½ tablespoons vinegar
1 pound lean pork, coarsely ground
¼ pound pork fat, coarsely ground
Sausage casings and string

Linguica is now available in a few area markets—but during the time when it was not, I devised this recipe.

———

Mix salt, pepper, paprika, rosemary, garlic, and vinegar. Knead pork and pork fat together. Mix in vinegar mixture. Stuff meat mixture firmly into casings and tie into 6-inch lengths with string. Prick any air pockets with a pin. Refrigerate for 1 to 3 days before using in soup. To store, package airtight and freeze for up to 3 months.

Makes about six 8-inch sausages.

Golden Herbed Pretzel Knots

1 envelope active dry yeast
1¼ cups lukewarm water
(about 110°F)
1 teaspoon salt
¼ cup vegetable oil
5 cups bread flour
Melted butter
¼ cup mixed snipped fresh
dill, chives, and parsley

These are perfect for dunking in any hearty soup. If you like, sprinkle the pretzels with sesame seeds, poppy seeds, or coarse salt instead of herbs.

———

In a large bowl, dissolve yeast in lukewarm water and let stand for 5 minutes. Add salt, then add oil and flour. Mix until dough becomes shiny. Then turn dough out onto a floured marble slab or flat surface and knead until no longer sticky (about 10 minutes). Place in an oiled bowl, cover with a warm, damp towel, and let rise in a warm place until doubled in bulk (about 40 minutes).

Punch down dough and divide into 12 equal portions. Roll each into a ¼-inch-thick, 12-inch-long rope. Twist ropes into pretzel knots and place on a greased baking sheet. Cover with a warm, damp towel and let rise in a warm place until doubled in bulk (about 40 minutes). Meanwhile, preheat oven to 425°F.

Brush pretzels with melted butter. Sprinkle with herbs. Bake in preheated oven until golden brown (about 20 minutes). Wrap in foil to keep warm.

Makes 1 dozen pretzels.

Apple Cake with Hot Rum Sauce

1 cup all-purpose flour
1 teaspoon baking soda
½ teaspoon ground cinnamon
½ teaspoon ground nutmeg
1 cup sugar
¼ cup butter, softened
1 egg
3 medium tart apples, peeled,
*   cored, and chopped*
½ cup chopped nuts
Hot Rum Sauce (recipe
*   follows) or whipped cream*

A wonderful and warm aromatic apple cake—perfect for fall evenings, and very simple to make. I love the flavor of the Hot Rum Sauce, but the cake is just as scrumptious smothered with brandy-laced whipped cream. My first landlady in Rochester, Minnesota, shared this recipe with me, and it's been a favorite ever since.

———

Preheat oven to 325°F. Butter a 9-inch-square baking pan. Combine flour, baking soda, cinnamon, and nutmeg. Set aside. In a large bowl, cream sugar and butter with an electric mixer until light and fluffy. Add egg. Slowly add dry ingredients. With a spoon, mix in apples and nuts. Spoon into prepared pan. Bake in preheated oven until a wooden pick or cake tester inserted in center of cake comes out clean (about 1 hour). Cool slightly before slicing; or wrap baking pan in foil for transport to picnic site. Serve warm, topped with Hot Rum Sauce or whipped cream.

Makes 12 servings.

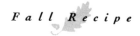

HOT RUM SAUCE
½ *cup packed brown sugar*
½ *cup sugar*
½ *cup half-and-half*
¼ *cup butter*
1 *to* 2 *tablespoons rum*

In a saucepan, bring sugars, half-and-half, and butter to a boil. Boil for 4 to 5 minutes, stirring often. Remove from heat and cool slightly. Add rum. Transport sauce to picnic site in a small thermos. Spoon 1 tablespoon sauce over each serving of warm apple cake.

NOTE: Rum extract may be substituted for rum.

An Herbal Gathering for 12

Deviled Chicken Breasts *
Pasta Salad
Herbed Cheese Focaccia *
Tarragon Mousse *
Herb Tea Punch

Whenever possible, use freshly picked herbs, which have a more intense flavor. But if you must dry some to use for winter cooking or tea-making, pick the sprigs just before they bloom. One teaspoon of dried herbs equals about three teaspoons fresh. Delicate herbs, such as tarragon, chervil, and dill, can be better preserved by blanching a small bundle in boiling water for a few seconds, draining, and then freezing.

For your pasta salad, be as creative as our many local caterers and deli chefs are. I've had fun creating a pasta salad with fruit and nuts and one with different hot and cold ethnic variations (Greek, German, or Japanese) as well as the standard Italian olives, artichokes, and provolone cheese. Just be sure to sprinkle the pasta with fresh herbs.

DEVILED CHICKEN BREASTS

3 tablespoons olive oil
1 cup pickled mushrooms,
   drained and chopped
3 tablespoons Dijon mustard
1 teaspoon Worcestershire
   sauce
6 large whole chicken breasts,
   skinned and split

Don't let the unattractive dark brown color dissuade you—the deviled coating for this chicken tastes great.

———

Mix oil, mushrooms, mustard, and Worcestershire sauce to form a paste. Spread half the paste in a very large glass dish; top with chicken breasts in a single layer. Cover with remaining paste; cover and refrigerate for 4 to 6 hours.

Preheat oven to 350°F. Bake chicken, uncovered, in preheated oven for 20 minutes. Cover dish and transport to picnic site. About 40 minutes before you are ready to eat, ignite coals and burn until white-hot. Grill chicken pieces 4 to 6 inches from coals until meat near bone is no longer pink (about 10 minutes per side).

Makes 12 servings.

HERBED CHEESE FOCACCIA

1 envelope active dry yeast
1 cup lukewarm water (about 110°F)
1 teaspoon salt
3 to 3¼ cups bread flour
Olive oil
Cornmeal
⅓ cup chopped fresh tarragon or rosemary
½ cup grated white Cheddar or Asiago cheese

If you've yet to taste this wonderful flat Italian bread, be warned: it is addictive. Those who don't have time to make their own focaccia can buy it in several area markets.

———

In a small bowl, dissolve yeast in lukewarm water and let stand for 5 minutes. In a large bowl, combine salt and 2½ cups of the flour. Stir in yeast mixture and 1 tablespoon olive oil. Turn dough out onto a floured marble slab or flat surface; knead until no longer sticky (about 10 minutes), working in ½ to ¾ cup more flour.

Place dough in an oiled bowl, cover with a warm, damp towel, and let rise in a warm place until doubled in bulk (45 to 60 minutes). Punch down. Cover and let rise for 45 to 60 more minutes. Punch down again, then let rest for 10 minutes.

Preheat oven to 475°F. Oil a 10-by-15-inch jelly-roll pan and dust with cornmeal. On pan, form dough into desired shape. How about 2 hearts or a large ring?

Cover dough and let rise in a warm place for 30 minutes. Flatten and dimple top with your fingers. Combine 1 tablespoon olive oil with herbs and brush lightly over dough. Sprinkle with cheese. Bake in preheated oven until golden (about 10 minutes). Serve warm or cold. To serve warm, wrap in foil to transport to picnic. If made in advance, wrap cooled bread airtight and store for up to 3 days. Reheat before serving, if desired.

Makes 12 servings.

TARRAGON MOUSSE

¾ *cup dry white wine*

3 *tablespoons chopped fresh*
  tarragon

1 *cup sugar*

6 *egg yolks*

¼ *teaspoon grated lemon peel*

1 *tablespoon fresh lemon*
  juice

1 *cup whipping cream*

Tarragon sprigs

2 *cups fresh strawberries,*
  rinsed, hulled, and drained
  (optional)

An elegant and delicious herbal dessert. The flavor isn't at all what most people expect.

———

In a 2-quart saucepan, combine wine and chopped tarragon. Add sugar, bring to a gentle boil, and boil gently until mixture registers 220°F on a candy thermometer. Place egg yolks in the top of a double boiler. Beat yolks to blend; gradually pour hot syrup into yolks, beating constantly with an electric mixer. Set over simmering water and cook, beating constantly, until mixture holds soft peaks (about 10 minutes). Remove from heat. Set top of double boiler over a pan of ice water and continue to beat egg mixture until cool. Stir in lemon peel and lemon juice.

In a chilled bowl, beat cream until stiff. Fold into egg mixture. Cover and freeze until firm (at least 6 hours) or for up to 1 month. Transport to picnic site in a cooler next to ice or a cold pack. Before serving, decorate with tarragon sprigs and, if desired, strawberries.

Makes 12 servings.

NOTE: One package whipped topping mix made with skim milk may be substituted for whipped cream.

TEDDY BEARS' PICNIC FOR 2
(PLUS 1 BEAR)

Nut Butter Sandwiches
Nuts and Berries
Orange Madeleines *
Milk, Tea, and Honey
Cider

An outing planned just for you, your favorite preschooler, and his or her Number One Bear. The picnic basket must be packed with selections appropriate to your bear-guest's appetite, of course. For a change, try almond or hazelnut butter instead of peanut butter on your sandwiches.

You might wish to make a stop at a favorite local emporium as part of this special picnic outing. Bazaar des Bears at 1909 First Avenue near the Pike Place Market is delightful. There you will find all manner of bear treasures plus bear greeting cards and books about bear travel adventures, designed and written by the store's owner.

Crabtree and Evelyn in Westlake Center and Bellevue Square sells a box of treats especially designed for a teddy bear picnic.

ORANGE MADELEINES

¾ cup butter
2 eggs
¾ cup sugar
1 tablespoon orange flower
water
½ teaspoon grated orange
peel
½ teaspoon vanilla
1 cup all-purpose flour
Powdered sugar

Tiny, shell-shaped cakes such as these were made famous by the French author Marcel Proust in his *Remembrance of Things Past.* The flavor of madeleines and lime-flower tea triggered Proust's long recollections of his youth.

French or Lebanese orange flower water is available at Larry's Markets and DeLaurenti's at the Pike Place Market.

Preheat oven to 450°F. Butter insides of madeleine molds.

Next, clarify butter: Cut it into small pieces and place in a small saucepan. Heat over low heat until foam disappears from top and sediment settles to bottom (about 10 minutes). Remove from heat. Pour clear liquid into a small bowl to cool, leaving sediment in saucepan.

Mix eggs, sugar, orange flower water, and orange peel in the top of a double boiler. Heat over simmering water, stirring often, until mixture is lukewarm (5 to 10 minutes). Remove from heat and beat with an electric mixer at high speed until light and fluffy. Add vanilla. Fold in flour and cooled clarified butter.

Fill madeleine molds two-thirds full with batter. Bake in preheated

oven until golden brown (7 to 8 minutes). Cool in molds for 2 minutes, then remove. Re-butter molds; refill with batter and bake. Repeat until all batter has been baked. Dust madeleines with powdered sugar. Store in an airtight container.

Makes about 40 madeleines.

BITE BACK THE COLD FOR 8

Hearty Chili *
Cheesy Johnny Bread *
Raw Vegetable Sticks
Apple Pie
Spiced Hot Chocolate *

A meal meant to fortify you and your guests against the cold. Each item is easily prepared ahead of time. For my apple pies, I try to find old, hearty varieties. I keep hoping I'll come across the same type of juicy winter apple that grew in my backyard when I was young. There, my sisters and I had our pick of six different varieties. One tree even had three types of apple and one pear grafted onto its trunk.

For those days in late November when there's no time to bake a pie, A La Francaise bakery in University Village (524-9300) will reserve one of their three dozen limited edition apple tarts for you. They are made from the same apple variety (Colville Blanc d'Hiver) loved by Louis XIII, XIV, and Napoleon.

The bright yellow and red Ibara packages of Mexican spiced chocolate in shops at the Pike Place Market, QFC, and Larry's are a substitute for the spiced chocolate recipe in this menu.

HEARTY CHILI

1½ pounds lean ground beef
1 clove garlic, minced
2 cans (about 15 ounces
each) red kidney beans,
undrained
1 large can (28 ounces)
stewed tomatoes
2 cans (10¾ ounces each)
Campbell's tomato soup
3 celery stalks, diced
1 medium onion, diced
1 large green bell pepper,
seeded and diced
1 tablespoon chili powder
1 teaspoon salt
½ teaspoon freshly ground
black pepper

A robust winter meal, first made in my Grandmother Holz's cozy kitchen and then again in my mother's. I return to this chili again and again because it is neither overly elaborate nor too sweet.

———

In a wide frying pan, cook beef with garlic until browned. Drain off fat; set beef aside.

In a large soup kettle, combine remaining ingredients and heat gently. Add cooked beef. Bring to a simmer; then cover and simmer for 1 hour. If made in advance, cool; then cover and refrigerate for up to 1 week. Reheat before taking to picnic. To transport to picnic site, wrap kettle of hot chili in newspapers.

Makes 8 servings.

CHEESY JOHNNY BREAD

1 cup yellow cornmeal, plus a little to dust baking pan
1 cup all-purpose flour
4 teaspoons baking powder
1 teaspoon salt
2 eggs
1 cup nonfat buttermilk
¼ cup butter, melted
½ cup grated sharp Cheddar cheese

It's difficult to imagine a more perfect companion for chili.

———

Preheat oven to 425°F. Butter a 9-inch-square baking pan and dust with cornmeal. In a bowl, sift together 1 cup cornmeal, flour, baking powder, and salt. In another bowl, beat eggs lightly; add buttermilk, butter, and cheese. Add buttermilk mixture to dry ingredients, stirring only until evenly moistened. Pour into prepared pan. Bake in preheated oven until a wooden pick or cake tester inserted in center of bread comes out clean (20 to 25 minutes). Do not overbake. If made in advance, cool; then wrap airtight and store for up to 2 days. Reheat before picnic time; wrap in foil to keep warm for transport to picnic site.

Makes 8 servings.

SPICED HOT CHOCOLATE

2 quarts milk

2 bars (4 ounces each) sweet
cooking chocolate, broken
into pieces

½ cup finely ground blanched
almonds

4 cinnamon sticks (each 3 to
6 inches long) for
flavoring

8 cinnamon sticks (each 6
inches long) for stirring

Cinnamon and ground almonds add a Mexican flavor to these steaming mugs of hot chocolate.

———

In a large saucepan, combine milk, chocolate, almonds, and 4 cinnamon sticks. Heat, stirring constantly, until chocolate is melted and mixture is steaming hot; do not boil. Remove from heat and discard cinnamon sticks. Whisk until frothy. Pour into a thermos to transport to picnic site. Shake before serving; pour into mugs and provide cinnamon stick stirrers.

Makes 8 servings.

BOXING DAY RECOVERY FOR 8

Pork Pot Pie
or
Tangy Rarebit*
Buttermilk Cucumbers*
Individual Steamed Cranberry Puddings
with
Brandied Berry Hard Sauce*
Juicy Winter Apples
Porter, Hard Cider or Ale, and Brandy
Murchie's Tea

In Canada and Great Britain, Boxing Day is celebrated on the day after Christmas. In medieval times, it was set aside for distributing the contents of alms boxes to the poor; later, the name referred to the Christmas box used by servants, customers, and delivery men to collect gratuities from the wealthier classes. More recently, Boxing Day has been associated with the exhausting day-after-Christmas sales—hence the need for the "recovery" provided by a hearty picnic like this one.

TANGY RAREBIT

¼ cup butter, softened
8 thick slices French bread
½ cup dark ale or red wine
1 tablespoon herb-flavored or
*   balsamic vinegar*
8 thin slices rare deli beef
Prepared horseradish sauce or
*   English mustard*
Freshly ground black pepper
*   to taste*
½ pound Stilton cheese or
*   other pungent farm cheese,*
*   grated*

Not at all like the traditional Welsh rarebit, these are hearty open-faced beef and cheese sandwiches that bring the flavors and aromas of a British pub to your winter picnic. They may be prepared ahead of time, then reheated; you can also serve them cold.

———

Spread butter over one side of each bread slice. Mix ale or wine with vinegar. Lightly sprinkle bread with mixture. Top each bread slice with a beef slice, then with horseradish sauce or mustard. Season with pepper. Cover with grated cheese. Sprinkle again with ale-vinegar mixture. Wrap in foil to transport to picnic. To serve hot, open up foil to expose tops of sandwiches; place on a grill and heat until cheese is melted. To serve cold, broil until cheese is melted before leaving for picnic; wrap in foil and transport to picnic.

Makes 8 servings.

BUTTERMILK CUCUMBERS

2 cucumbers
1 tablespoon salt
½ cup milk
2 tablespoons white vinegar

This dish has been a favorite of mine ever since I was a child. It is refreshing and easy to make.

———

Wash cucumbers, then score lengthwise with a fork. Thinly slice crosswise. Place in a large bowl and cover with cold water; stir in salt. Cover and refrigerate overnight. Drain. Mix milk and vinegar and pour over cucumber slices. Transport to picnic in a glass jar with a lid.

Makes 8 servings.

INDIVIDUAL STEAMED CRANBERRY PUDDINGS WITH BRANDIED BERRY HARD SAUCE

*2 cups fresh or frozen
  cranberries, chopped*
1/2 cup chopped nuts
1/4 cup orange-flavored liqueur
2 eggs
1 1/3 cups all-purpose flour
1 teaspoon baking soda
1/2 teaspoon salt
1/2 cup butter, softened
1/2 cup sugar
1/2 cup dark molasses
*2 teaspoons grated orange
  peel*
*Brandied Berry Hard Sauce
  (recipe follows)*

Cranberries add a tangy flavor to these little puddings.

———

In a bowl, combine cranberries, nuts, and liqueur; let soak for 30 minutes while preparing other ingredients. Also remove eggs from refrigerator and bring to room temperature; then separate and set aside.

Preheat oven to 350°F. Butter twelve 1½-cup oven-proof containers. Mix flour, baking soda, and salt. Set aside. In a large bowl, cream butter and sugar until light and fluffy. Beat in molasses, egg yolks, and orange peel. Add flour mixture alternately with cranberry-nut mixture, mixing well after each addition.

In a clean bowl, beat egg whites until stiff; fold into batter. Pour into prepared containers. Cover each tightly with foil and place in a large baking pan. Pour boiling water around containers to 1-inch level. Bake in preheated oven until a wooden pick or cake tester inserted in center of puddings comes out clean (about 25 minutes).

Meanwhile, prepare Brandied Berry Hard Sauce.

Wrap puddings in foil for transport to picnic site; serve sauce over puddings. If puddings are prepared in advance, cool; wrap airtight and refrigerate for up to 2 weeks. Reheat, wrapped in foil, before transporting to picnic.

Makes 1 dozen individual puddings (12 servings).

BRANDIED BERRY HARD SAUCE
½ cup fresh or frozen cranberries
¼ cup sugar
¼ cup water
1 cup butter, softened
2 cups powdered sugar, sifted
1 teaspoon vanilla
¼ cup brandy

In a saucepan, bring cranberries, sugar, and water to a boil over high heat. Reduce heat, cover, and simmer for 10 minutes. Remove from heat. Mash cranberries, stirring to blend. Cool completely.

In a bowl, cream butter and powdered sugar until light and fluffy. Add vanilla, brandy, and cranberry mixture. Return to saucepan and reheat gently. Transport to picnic site in a small thermos.

Snow Play Warm-Up for 4

Penn Cove Mussel Soup *
Finger Vegetables
Crusty Farmhouse Bread
Ruby Red Cake *
Hot Mulled Port
Hot Spiced Cranberry Juice

After a hard day of inner-tubing or cross-country skiing, you and your companions will need to replenish spent calories. This hearty menu will do the trick.

Hot mulled port can be blended with a prepared mix or your own invention. Gently heat the port with citrus slices, cinnamon sticks, nutmeg, whole nuts, and raisins. Then, at the sleigh-riding hill, pour a mugful from your thermos and warm your hands. Be sure to include spoons to scoop up the leftover fruit and nuts.

PENN COVE MUSSEL SOUP

48 mussels (12 per person)
1 cup rosé or white wine
1 onion, chopped
3 stalks celery, chopped
1 tablespoon chopped parsley
2 cloves garlic, minced
1 tomato, chopped
1 teaspoon cornstarch
½ teaspoon garlic powder
1 teaspoon each chopped
   fresh tarragon, basil, and
   thyme leaves
½ cup dry sherry
½ cup rosé or white wine
½ cup Whidbeys Port Wine

This recipe was inspired by a heavenly velvet broth created by Ruth Simon in her 100-year-old home on Windy Hill across from Whidbey Island's Penn Cove. It's the perfect warm-up to share with close friends on a crisp winter day.

———

Wash mussels in clean salt water. Check to see if mussels are alive by tapping shells: the shells should close when tapped as well as resist your attempts to pry them apart. The mussels should smell as fresh and sweet as Penn Cove.

Remove mussel "beards" (byssus threads) that protrude from the concave side of shells by trimming them off with scissors or pulling sharply on them. Be careful not to cut your hands on threads.

Layer mussels in a large kettle no deeper than 8 inches. Add next 6 ingredients. Cover and bring to a rolling boil. Steam until mussels open (3 to 5 minutes), then turn off heat. Discard any unopened mussels.

Remove mussels from kettle and strain broth, discarding cooked vegetables. Return strained mussel broth to kettle; add remaining ingredients, stirring after each addition. Remove steamed mussels

from shells, if you wish; then return to kettle and heat gently. If made in advance, cool; then cover and refrigerate for up to 3 days. Reheat gently before taking to picnic. Transport to picnic site in a large thermos or wide-mouth insulated picnic jug.

Makes 4 servings.

RUBY RED CAKE

3 eggs
1 cup boiling water
3 squares (3 ounces)
semisweet chocolate,
broken into pieces
1¼ teaspoons baking soda
½ cup butter, softened
1½ cups sugar
½ teaspoon salt
2½ cups sifted cake flour
1 cup sour cream
1 teaspoon red food coloring
1 teaspoon vanilla
½ cup sugar
Fudge Frosting (recipe
follows)

Many years ago when I was a student nurse in Rochester, Minnesota, the wife of a patient shared this recipe with me. I have yet to taste its equal. It is so moist and rich, you'll think you're nibbling the $300 Red Velvet Cake at the Waldorf-Astoria.

———

Remove eggs from refrigerator and bring to room temperature; then separate and set aside.

Preheat oven to 325°F. Butter two 9-inch cake pans and dust with flour.

In a small bowl, pour boiling water over broken chocolate; let stand until chocolate is melted. Add baking soda. In a large bowl, cream butter and 1½ cups sugar with an electric mixer until light and fluffy. Beat in egg yolks and salt. Add flour alternately with sour cream, beating thoroughly after each addition. Add food coloring, vanilla, and melted chocolate mixture. Beat well.

In a clean bowl, beat egg whites until stiff; then gradually beat in ½ cup sugar. Fold into cake batter. Pour into prepared pans. Bake in preheated oven until a wooden pick or cake tester inserted in center of cake comes out clean (about 25 minutes). Cool briefly in pans, then turn out onto cake racks to cool completely. Prepare Fudge Frosting and ice cake.

Makes 12 servings.

FUDGE FROSTING
2 squares (2 ounces) semisweet chocolate, broken into pieces
5 tablespoons milk
¼ cup butter
1 pound powdered sugar, sifted
1 teaspoon vanilla

In a saucepan, combine chocolate, milk, and butter; heat over low heat, stirring, until chocolate is melted. Gradually add powdered sugar and vanilla and mix well. If frosting is too thick, add a little more milk.

A SAMPLING OF SAVORIES FOR 12

Crisp Snow Peas
with
Anchovy Dip*
Marinated Cheese with Roasted Peppers
Nutwood* with Toast
Sweet Potato Crisps with Lemon Pepper*
Seed Cake*
Claret
Tea

A quickly assembled picnic of easily prepared nibbles. If you delegate the preparation of each item on the menu to one of your guests, you can concentrate on finding the ideal site and the perfect decorations.

Snow peas are available year-round in Seattle. If you cannot find them where you live, substitute crisp carrot, jicama, or turnip spears.

Marinated fresh mozzarella balls with roasted bell peppers are available as a take-out item in local delis.

ANCHOVY DIP

2 egg yolks
3 to 4 tablespoons Dijon
mustard
1 can (2 ounces) anchovies,
undrained
Juice of 1 lemon
1 shallot, chopped
1 cup olive oil
Salt and freshly ground black
pepper to taste
1 tablespoon capers, rinsed,
drained, and chopped
(reserve a few whole capers
for garnish)
1¼ pounds snow peas, rinsed,
drained, and destringed

This is the perfect coating for crisp snow peas. It's enjoyed even by those who avoid anchovies, since the tiny, heavily salted fish don't overwhelm the flavor. To serve, arrange the washed, crisped pea pods in a sunburst, centered with a silver bowl of cold dip.

To give the flavors time to blend, prepare this dip at least 3 days before your picnic.

———

Combine first 5 ingredients in a food processor or blender (or in a bowl). Process (or beat with an electric mixer) until foamy and pale yellow (about 10 minutes). While still processing or beating, gradually drizzle in oil in a slow, steady stream until entirely absorbed. Season to taste with salt and pepper. Stir in chopped capers; cover and refrigerate for at least 3 days or up to 2 weeks. When ready to serve, garnish with reserved whole capers.

Makes 1½ cups (12 servings)

NOTE: This sauce can be thinned with champagne vinegar, seasoned with garlic, and used as a dressing for salads or fish.

NUTWOOD

2 cups grated sharp Cheddar
cheese
½ cup finely chopped toasted,
skinned hazelnuts
½ cup finely chopped dried
fruit, such as apples,
apricots, golden raisins,
cherries, or pears
½ cup nonalcoholic cider

In an old cookery book, I read a description of an English cheese so intriguing that I couldn't resist devising my own version of this slightly sweetened spread.

———

In a bowl, blend all ingredients well with a spoon. Transfer to an opaque crock or small bowl; cover until ready to serve. If made in advance, refrigerate for up to 1 week, but bring to room temperature before serving; nutwood has a tendency to crumble when cold.

Makes 2 cups (12 servings).

SWEET POTATO CRISPS
WITH LEMON PEPPER

*6 medium sweet potatoes or
   yams, peeled*
Canola oil
Lemon pepper

A savory new twist on the familiar potato chip.

———

In a wide, heavy skillet, heat 2 inches of oil to 350°F. Thinly slice potatoes. Carefully drop slices, a handful at a time, into hot oil. Cook until slices rise to top of oil and turn light brown (about 4 minutes). Drain on paper towels. Sprinkle with lemon pepper. As you cook, be careful to maintain oil temperature at 350°F. Keep crisps in a tightly covered container until ready to serve.

Makes 12 servings.

SEED CAKE

1½ cups all-purpose flour
1¼ teaspoons baking powder
½ teaspoon salt
½ teaspoon ground mace
½ teaspoon ground
  cardamom
⅓ cup butter, softened
1 cup sugar
2 tablespoons chopped
  lemon peel
2 eggs
½ cup nonfat buttermilk
1½ teaspoons poppy seeds
½ teaspoon anise seeds
2 teaspoons plus a pinch of
  caraway seeds

A popular teatime choice for centuries, this cake is the perfect partner for claret, sherry, or port. Serve warm, with warmed English lemon curd.

———

Preheat oven to 350°F. Butter a fluted 8½-inch bundt pan and dust with flour.

Mix flour, baking powder, salt, mace, and cardamom; set aside.

In a large bowl, cream butter and sugar with an electric mixer until light and fluffy. Add lemon peel; then add eggs, one at a time, beating well after each addition. Gradually add flour mixture alternately with buttermilk, beating well after each addition. Combine poppy seeds, anise seeds, and 2 teaspoons of the caraway seeds; stir into batter. Pour into prepared pan and smooth top. Sprinkle with a pinch of caraway seeds.

Bake in preheated oven until a wooden pick or cake tester inserted in center of cake comes out clean (about 1 hour). Cool in pan for 15 minutes, then turn out of pan. Wrap whole cake, or just portions needed, in foil for transport to picnic.

Makes 12 servings.

Sugarplums and Nutcrackers for 24

Fried Nuts *
Creamy Caramels *
Dried Figs, Cherries, and Apricots
Almond Crescents *
Nuts in the Shell
Strawberry Wine
Thick Eggnog *
Coffee

This is the type of picnic that requires a little forethought and planning. First, reserve an enclosed picnic lodge or park shelter like those you'll find at the Arboretum, the Center for Urban Horticulture, and Lincoln Park. To enhance the holiday mood, have a recording of the *Nutcracker Suite* playing in the background. If you're blessed, a layer of snow may fall and encourage smooth cross-country gliding before it's time to eat. Finally, spread this magical dessert buffet before your rosy-cheeked guests.

Wine that recaptures the fresh flavor of strawberries is fast becoming a Northwest holiday tradition. Reserve your bottles of Bainbridge Island Winery's gold-medal strawberry wine before the end of June by calling (206) 842-WINE (9643). You'll need to travel to the winery between November 14 and December 8 to collect your purchase.

FRIED NUTS

1½ quarts water
4 cups whole shelled nuts
½ cup sugar
Canola (rapeseed) oil
Salt

You will have a hard time keeping these around. Experiment by using different nuts and a variety of seasonings, such as curry powder.

At least 1½ hours before the picnic, pour water into a 4-quart saucepan and bring to a boil. Add nuts and return to a boil; boil for 1 minute. Rinse nuts under hot running water. Drain. Wash saucepan and dry well.

In a large bowl, gently mix warm nuts and sugar with a wooden spoon until sugar is dissolved. If necessary, let stand to finish dissolving sugar.

In washed, dried saucepan, heat 1 inch of oil to 350°F. With a slotted spoon, add about half the nuts. Cook until golden (about 15 minutes), stirring often. Place nuts in a strainer over a bowl to drain. Sprinkle lightly with salt. Stir. Cool on wax paper. Repeat with remaining nuts. Store in a tightly covered container for up to 2 weeks.

Makes 4 cups (24 servings).

CREAMY CARAMELS

4½ cups sugar
1½ cups light corn syrup
1½ quarts whipping cream
1½ cups chopped pecans
1 tablespoon vanilla

At the convent school I attended, Sister Lucy's caramels were a Christmas tradition and often given as the choice prize in academic contests.

———

Butter a 9-by-13-inch pan. In a 2-gallon kettle, mix sugar, corn syrup, and 2 cups of the cream. Bring mixture to a boil; boil until mixture registers 235°F (soft ball stage) on a candy thermometer (about 30 minutes). Slowly drizzle in 2 cups more cream, making sure to keep mixture boiling. Then slowly add remaining 2 cups cream, and boil to 240°F (firm ball stage), wearing oven mitts and stirring gently and constantly with a long-handled wooden spoon (this will take about 30 minutes).

Remove kettle from heat at 240°F. Stir in pecans and vanilla and pour into prepared pan. Cover with plastic wrap and refrigerate. When cold, cut into 1-inch-square pieces and wrap individually.

Makes about 10 dozen pieces.

ALMOND CRESCENTS

1 cup butter, softened
¼ cup powdered sugar
1½ teaspoons almond extract
2¼ cups all-purpose flour
½ cup blanched almonds,
  toasted and finely chopped
Powdered sugar

These buttery morsels are found in a slightly different version in nearly every country.

————

Preheat oven to 325°F.

In a large bowl, cream butter and ¼ cup powdered sugar until light and fluffy. Add almond extract, then flour. Mix well. Stir in almonds. Shape level teaspoonfuls of dough into crescent shapes on ungreased baking sheets. Bake in preheated oven until lightly browned (25 to 30 minutes). Remove from baking sheets and cool on a rack for 5 minutes, then coat in powdered sugar. Transfer to an airtight container for storage and transport to picnic site.

Makes about 5 dozen cookies.

THICK EGGNOG

6 large eggs
1 cup sugar
½ cup brandy
½ cup rum
3 cups whipping cream
3 cups whole milk
Whole nutmeg, freshly grated

This rich, velvety nog is the perfect libation to toast the Yule. Use the best brandy and rum you can afford and watch the plush mustaches form on your guests' upper lips.

———

One to 2 days before serving, remove eggs from refrigerator and bring to room temperature; then separate. Refrigerate egg whites in a tightly covered container until next day. In a large bowl, beat egg yolks with ¾ cup of the sugar, using an electric mixer at high speed until thick and lemon-colored (about 8 minutes). Add ¼ cup *each* of the brandy and rum. Pour into a noncorrodible container. Cover and refrigerate overnight.

On picnic day, remove egg whites from refrigerator and bring to room temperature. In deep, narrow bowl, beat egg whites until softly mounded. Continue to beat until peaks form, gradually adding 2 more tablespoons of the sugar. Transfer to a covered container and refrigerate until ready to transport to picnic site.

Refrigerate a large mixer bowl and beaters. In chilled bowl, beat cream until it begins to thicken. Gradually add remaining 2 tablespoons sugar and beat until cream holds stiff peaks. Transfer to a covered container and refrigerate until ready to transport to picnic site.

At the picnic site, pour egg yolk mixture into 6-quart punch bowl.

Whisk in remaining ¼ cup *each* brandy and rum; then whisk in milk. Slide in whipped cream.

Fold egg whites into mixture. Continue folding cream, whites, and eggnog together until mixed but still fluffy.

Sprinkle with fresh nutmeg. Enjoy! Celebrate! Toast the Yule!

Makes 24 servings.

WINTER SOLSTICE FOR 10

Northwest Fish Chowder *
Best of Oregon Tossed Salad *
Onion Bread
Loganberry Port Frozen Cream *
Hot Market Spice Tea

There are many arguments in favor of getting out into the Northwest winter and creating a memorable picnic. Presenting our outstanding regional foods in new ways is the most compelling reason I can think of.

Hot mugs of bottomfish and mussels in a buttery broth; pickled cranberries, hazelnuts, and goat cheese in a mixed green salad; bits of roasted onion in steaming hunks of bread; and a dessert of Whidbeys Port Wine, all combine to make a colorful and warming contrast to your guests' clouds of breath and snow-sprinkled caps.

NORTHWEST FISH CHOWDER

1 quart water

*2 pounds mussels, cleaned (see
page 169), butter clams,
geoducks, scallops, or prawns*

½ cup dry white wine

1 lemon, sliced

6 slices bacon, cut up

*2 small leeks, trimmed, cleaned,
and slivered*

4 scallions, slivered

2 cloves garlic, minced

*1 small green bell pepper,
roasted, peeled, seeded, and
cut into strips*

2 tablespoons all-purpose flour

*2 bottles (8 ounces each) clam
juice*

*3 medium red thin-skinned
potatoes, scrubbed and cubed*

*1 pound firm whitefish, cut into
chunks*

*1 cucumber, peeled, seeded, and
chopped*

2 cups nonfat buttermilk

2 teaspoons cornstarch

1 teaspoon salt

White pepper to taste

¼ teaspoon hot pepper sauce

On an Indian summer afternoon at Thom and Jan Gunn's Whidbey's Fish Barbecue and Market in the town of Greenbank, I sampled the most memorable chowder I have ever tasted. Ever since, I've tried to create my own award-winner by experimenting with various ingredients. I encourage you to do the same. The fish and shellfish you add will naturally vary with the season.

———

In a 5-quart soup kettle, bring water to a boil. Reduce heat and add shellfish, wine, and lemon slices. Cover and steam until shells open (or until prawns turn pink) — about 5 minutes. Discard any unopened shells. Strain broth; return to kettle. Remove meat from shells and mince; or shell and devein prawns, then mince. Add to broth.

In a frying pan, cook bacon until lightly browned and crisp. Remove with a slotted metal spoon and

drain on paper towels. Pour off and discard all but 2 tablespoons of the drippings.

Add leeks, scallions, garlic, and pepper strips to reserved 2 table-spoons drippings in pan; cook over medium heat until softened. Add flour and stir until lightly browned. Stir in clam juice.

Add vegetable–clam juice mixture to shellfish broth in kettle. Add potatoes, whitefish, cucumber, buttermilk, and cornstarch. Bring to a simmer; cover and simmer until potatoes and fish are tender (about 15 minutes). Add salt, pepper, and hot pepper sauce. Simmer for 10 more minutes.

Transport soup to picnic site in a wide-mouth insulated picnic jug.

Makes 10 servings.

BEST OF OREGON TOSSED SALAD

*Cranberry Vinaigrette
(recipe follows)*
*½ cup fresh cranberries,
cut up*
*1 quart washed, crisped
mixed salad greens, such
as romaine or leaf lettuce,
Belgian endive, and
arugula, torn into bite-
size pieces*
½ cup julienned celery
½ cup julienned jicama
*½ small purple onion, sliced
and separated into rings*
*1 to 2 ounces Oregon Bleu
cheese, crumbled*
*4 to 6 ounces Oregon shrimp
(optional)*
*1 tablespoon chopped toasted,
skinned hazelnuts*

Oregon's famous foods meld perfectly to create an exciting, piquant salad.

———

Prepare Cranberry Vinaigrette. Pour a small amount of the vinaigrette over cut-up cranberries; let stand for 2 hours. Refrigerate remaining vinaigrette until you are ready to leave for the picnic. Mix remaining ingredients in a large bowl and refrigerate until time to transport to picnic.

To serve, add marinated cranberries to salad bowl. Then drizzle remaining vinaigrette sparingly over salad; toss to mix.

Makes 10 servings.

CRANBERRY VINAIGRETTE
¼ cup cranberry vinegar
¼ teaspoon paprika
Pinch of cayenne pepper
1 clove garlic, minced
6 tablespoons nut or vegetable oil

Combine all ingredients in a cruet or screw-top jar and shake well.
Refrigerate. Shake again before using.

NOTE: If you cannot find cranberry vinegar, simply crush a few
cranberries in ¼ cup white wine vinegar, shake, and let stand for at
least 15 minutes or until ready to use. Capers may be substituted for
pickled cranberries.

LOGANBERRY PORT FROZEN CREAM

1 cup lowfat cottage cheese
1 tablespoon fresh lemon
juice
½ cup sugar
1 cup sour cream
½ to ¾ cup Whidbey's
Port Wine
Green leaves and frozen
loganberries (thawed)

This is a rich dessert, so small servings are sufficient. You can use the mixture as the filling for a frozen pie, too.

———

Place cottage cheese in a cheesecloth, set over a bowl, and let drain for 1 hour; then twist cloth firmly around cheese to extract all liquid. Discard liquid. In a blender, blend cottage cheese until smooth (or beat with an electric mixer). Add lemon juice and sugar and blend well; add sour cream and blend. With blender or mixer running, gradually drizzle in port until entirely absorbed.

Turn mixture into a metal ice cube tray and freeze until firm around edges (about 1 hour). Transfer to a chilled bowl and beat with an electric mixer until smooth. Return to tray, cover tightly, and freeze until firm (about 3 hours) or for up to 1 month.

Transport to picnic site in a cooler next to ice or a cold pack. To serve, scoop into small bowls; garnish with leaves and loganberries.

Makes 10 servings.

NOTE: You may substitute imitation sour cream for the dairy sour cream.

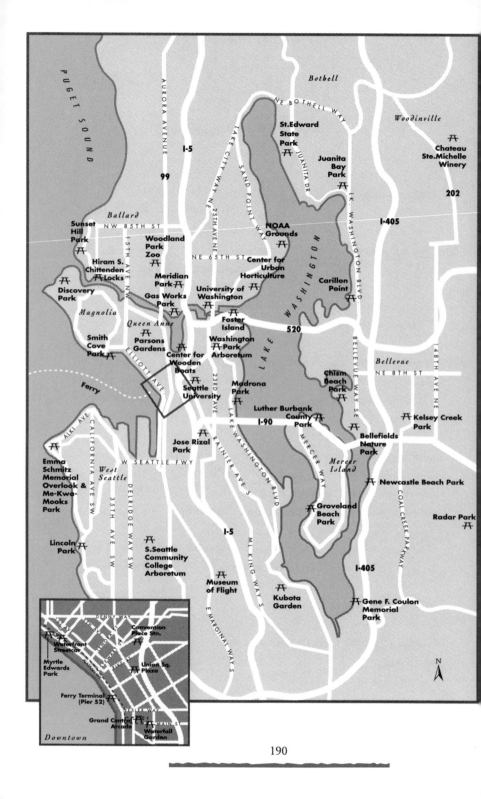

PUGET SOUND

Bothell

Woodinville

AURORA AVENUE

I-5

99

NE BOTHELL WAY

St. Edward State Park

LAKE CITY WAY NE

SAND POINT WAY

25TH AVE NE

JUANITA DR

Juanita Bay Park

LK WASHINGTON BLVD.

Chateau Ste. Michelle Winery

I-405

202

Ballard

Sunset Hill Park

NW 85TH ST

15TH AVE NW

Woodland Park Zoo

NE 65TH ST

NOAA Grounds

Center for Urban Horticulture

Hiram S. Chittenden Locks

Meridian Park

Gas Works Park

University of Washington

Carillon Point

LAKE WASHINGTON

Discovery Park

Magnolia

Smith Cove Park

Queen Anne

Parsons Gardens

Foster Island

Washington Park Arboretum

520

Bellevue

NE 8TH ST

148TH AVE NE

ELLIOTT AVE

Center for Wooden Boats

Seattle University

Madrona Park

Chism Beach Park

BELLEVUE WAY SE

Kelsey Creek Park

Ferry

Luther Burbank County Park

23RD AVE

I-90

Bellefields Nature Park

Jose Rizal Park

RAINIER AVE S

LAKE WASHINGTON BLVD

MERCER WAY

Mercer Island

Newcastle Beach Park

Emma Schmitz Memorial Overlook & Me-Kwa-Mooks Park

ALKI AVE

CALIFORNIA AVE SW

West Seattle

W SEATTLE FWY

35TH AVE SW

DELRIDGE WAY SW

Groveland Beach Park

COAL CREEK PKWY

Radar Park

Lincoln Park

S. Seattle Community College Arboretum

I-5

Museum of Flight

E MARGINAL WAY S

KING WAY S

Kubota Garden

I-405

Gene F. Coulon Memorial Park

DENNY WAY

Convention Place Stn.

Waterfront Streetcar

Myrtle Edwards Park

Union Sq. Plaza

Ferry Terminal (Pier 52)

Grand Central Arcade

MAIN ST.

Waterfall Garden

Downtown

N

PICNIC SITES

Seattle is a place where it is possible to picnic throughout the seasons. Here, each season possesses its own allure: the early fragrances and blossoms of spring; the just-picked berries and summer sun glistening on the city's ever-present waters; basil-bounty and crackling driftwood fires in fall; and in winter, the joy of sailing Puget Sound one day and carving the first cross-country trails through snow the next.

In carefully choosing the picnic sites, I assumed that one side of Lake Washington may know its own neighborhood well, but not necessarily the prime spots on the other side. You don't have to go very far to find a place you've never tried. If you spread out your map and mark the picnic spots selected, you will see they form a ring encircling Lake Washington. Each picnic site is within 45 minutes of downtown Seattle or Bellevue. I've attempted to construct a list that persuades even the most homebound persons to venture forth to places near them that are attractive and frequently underused. The area has such a remarkable range of topography—open beaches, dense forest, marshlands, quiet lakefronts, and an exciting urban core—and lends itself to a variety of experiences. If you have just arrived in the region, I hope this book will encourage you to explore these diverse sites.

My favorite spots to picnic appear in every corner of the greater Seattle area. In my list of suggested picnic sites, you'll discover a little-known Japanese garden in Rainier Valley; gracious chateau grounds in Woodinville where you can enjoy Shakespeare and a glass of wine; soaring views from a former Nike missile site in the Issaquah Alps far above the surrounding hills; and a hidden waterfall garden tucked in the corner of a downtown building. Whether you are planning a family reunion or a romantic outing for two, these selected sites should have broad appeal.

If you are planning a large group gathering between April 1 and September 30, you might want to reserve a picnic shelter at one of the Seattle parks. Reservations are accepted for three shelters at Gas Works Park, five shelters at Lincoln Park, one shelter at Madrona Park, one at Meridian Park, and one shelter at Jose Rizal Park. Reservations may be made with the Seattle Parks Department's Recreation Information Office at 5201 Green Lake Way North, beginning the first weekday in March. Most reservations are made on the first day they are accepted, so show up before the park office opens at 8:00 A.M. Reservations are also accepted by phone at 684-4081.

If you choose to travel to the picnic sites by bus, use the handy bus route numbers listed. They are the current routes that stop near each site after traveling from downtown Seattle. Call the Metro customer assistance number (447-4800) for their latest route information and schedules or if you plan to travel by bus from your home. Also, routes using the downtown tunnel are continually being revised.

Bus stops are not usually conveniently located next to the picnic sites. You should plan to walk a few blocks from the main arterials, so pack your picnic fare with that in mind.

For those of you who will use a car, I'd like to persuade you to purchase and keep readily available, in your trunk, grills, picnic containers, coolers, picnic blanket or ground cloth, and chairs. Gathering equipment should never be an impediment. Stock your freezer and shelves with labeled picnic fare; keep maps and a reminder list of delis and markets on your route home from work. The following list will help you be more spontaneous:

copy of *Seattle Picnics*
thermos, reusable food containers
cooler
ice, frozen cold packs, frozen milk cartons of water
hibachi, charcoal, matches, starter fluid
grill tools, hot pad

spray oil to coat grill

blankets, picnic rugs, reed mats, tablecloths

eating utensils

church key, cork screw, bottle opener

plates, cups

sun protection, sunglasses

detailed maps of cities and states of Northwest

folding beach rests, chairs

water and sand toys

first-aid kit

cheese slicer

sharp paring knife

towelettes, damp washcloth, lemon juice

paper towels

plastic bag for refuse

I hope that *Seattle Picnics* will inspire you to use these menu and site suggestions to create your own memorable Northwest traditions. Remember, "picnic" means a place, a taste, an outdoor excursion, and a relaxed approach to life—all rolled into one. Select your picnic fare and destinations from the list in *Seattle Picnics*, then all you need do is invite people whose company and conversation you enjoy, and set out for your outdoor adventure.

CENTER FOR WOODEN BOATS

A waterfront park and marina devoted to the wooden boat.

1010 Valley Street, Seattle.
382-2628

Located at the south end of
Lake Union. From I-5, take the
Mercer Street exit. At Fairview
Avenue North, turn right, and
then left onto Valley Street.
The parking lot for the Center
for Wooden Boats is on your
immediate right, between a
restaurant and the Naval
Reserve Training Center.

Hours: Daily, 11:00 A.M. to
7:00 P.M.
Water and restrooms are
available. No tables or
barbecues.
Fees: For boat rentals only.
Bus routes: 26, 28, 71, 72,
73, 305

The view of the shore lacks ladies
strolling with bustles and parasols
and gentlemen in bowlers and
spats, but the pavilion, boathouse,
and boat shop of the Center for
Wooden Boats are intended to
recall the Seattle lakeside of the
1900s. Those who yearn for a
maritime heritage park at the south
end of Lake Union would like to
see the return of lazy afternoons
on the water, lakeside picnics, and
the pavilion dances that were
popular at the turn of the century.

Dedicated to preserving traditional woodworking and boatbuilding skills required in the
design and construction of wooden
boats, the Center for Wooden
Boats is a living maritime museum. Nearly 100 vintage and replica
wooden rowboats and sailboats are on display in the water. Most are
available for rent for $8.00 to $25.00 an hour. (Little or no instruc-
tion is required for taking out the rowboats; you must demonstrate
your level of ability to rent the sailboats.) Boatbuilding and
woodworking classes and workshops are offered by the center;
visitors are often able to observe these activities. Volunteers (espe-

cially those skilled in woodworking) are always needed for restoration and maintenance work.

If you don't rent one of the boats for a picnic on the water, spread your picnic on the benches in the covered pavilion set on a landscaped bank overlooking the center and adjacent marina. Old dugout canoes and a Bristol Bay fishing boat hang from the rafters and allow close-up inspection of these craft.

In early July each year, the center hosts a wooden boat show that has been known to attract more than 30,000 enthusiasts.

Just to the west of the center, Northwest Seaport (open weekends only from 10:00 A.M. to 4:00 P.M.) will provide you with information on the 1893, three-masted Pacific schooner *Wawona*, moored just outside Northwest Seaport offices on Lake Union. The ship's restoration and moorage at a Lake Union maritime park was a dream of the late Seattle city councilman Wing Luke.

The *Wawona* first carried lumber in its hold, then codfish caught in the Bering Sea. It reverted once again to a lumber barge during World War II. Never having housed an engine, the ship was created and retired as a sailing vessel.

Sections of the *Wawona* not being worked on are open to the public during Northwest Seaport's office hours.

CONVENTION PLACE STATION

An open-air, paved square with grouped benches and planters.

Ninth Avenue between Olive and Pine in downtown Seattle. 447-4800 (Metro information)

Located north of downtown Seattle's retail core. Take the Stewart Street exit from I-5, turn left (south) on Ninth Avenue and drive two blocks.

Hours: Monday through Friday, 5:00 A.M. to 11:00 P.M.; Saturday, 10:00 A.M. to 6:00 P.M. The tunnel is closed on Sundays and holidays.
Water and restrooms are available. No tables or barbecues.
Fees: None
Bus routes: 71, 72, 73, 106, and 107 run through the tunnel. Other routes to be added in the future.

With the creation of the underground bus tunnel, Metro has provided an attractive urban gathering place at the Convention Place Station on the tunnel's north end. If you have a couple of hours some afternoon, your picnic could be the first phase of a trip through the tunnel to explore the artwork of the five stations.

The art and decor in each tunnel station are original, highly crafted, and express distinct themes. The stations make clear references to their neighborhoods and to Seattle life.

Begin your tour at the Convention Place Station. The open-air, paved square sits above and away from bus traffic. You can picnic on any of the white benches that line outdoor walls and surround huge concrete planters. Don't be put off by the concrete: on close inspection, this site reveals artistry and care. At the corner of Ninth and Pine streets, two modern neon marquees fashioned by New York sculptor Alice Adams echo the shape of the classic Paramount Theatre marquee across Pine Street.

197

Look for lyrics and a silhouette of Jimi Hendrix, who was born and raised in Seattle, under the marquee near the stairs.

Descend to the bus level at Convention Place to Bay C, "Southbound Routes and International District Station." All buses that travel in the tunnel stop at each station, so you can board any bus at Bay C. In addition, all tunnel stops are within the free-ride zone, so you may hop on and off with no fare worries. The bus waits are never very long.

The next stop, Westlake Station, is in the heart of the city's retail core. The mezzanine of the dazzling two-level concourse provides access to The Bon, Frederick & Nelson, Nordstrom, and Westlake Center. Art deco opulence is created by polished granite walls, patterned tiles, an architect-designed station clock, and detailed lighting fixtures. Three large, brightly colored murals cleverly portray the world of shopping and of city life.

The high-tech theme of the University Street Station is rendered in red, gray, and black. On the mezzanine level, light-works flash electronic messages, symbols, and depictions of technology. The artwork at the opposite end of this level seems from a distance to be vertical flashing lights. If you stand in front of the piece and let your eyes play across it, neon symbols and signs emerge, suggestive of the lights on Third Avenue.

The Pioneer Square station uses a theme of arches, vaulted ceilings, and ornate cast-iron gates relating to the district's landmark architecture. Clocks at either end of the station incorporate tools that helped construct the tunnel, as well as construction rubble. The pergola covering the Jefferson Street entrance echoes the one in Pioneer Square. Look for a mosaic-style mural on the wall near this entrance.

The International District Station combines motifs related to Asian culture and to the railroad. At the lower bus level, gridlike green window frames imitate the frames of the old Union Station nearby; and on the walls, eight large squares are filled with four-pointed origami designs, their folds a three-dimensional illusion. At street level, look for the twelve signs of the Chinese calendar rendered in rust, red, and brown inlaid brickwork. Near the Jackson Street entrance, colorful tiles set into a wall were created by Seattle schoolchildren.

DISCOVERY PARK

*View bluffs with meadow and woodland trails leading to beaches
and an old lighthouse.*

3801 West Government Way,
Seattle.
386-4236

Located south of Ballard on the
northwest corner of Magnolia.
From 15th Avenue NW in
Ballard, take the West Dravus
Street exit and head west. Turn
north (right) onto 27th Avenue
West. At West Tilden Street,
turn west (left) and drive one
block to West Emerson Street.
Turn right onto West Emerson
and drive to the south entrance
to the park.

Hours: Daily, 8:30 A.M. to dusk.
Tables, barbecues, water, and
    restrooms are available.
Bus routes: 24, 33

Beyond the entrances to Discovery Park, picnickers can experience a restorative wilderness close to the heart of the city. These grounds, once the Fort Lawton Army base, are so vast and diverse that a full exploration requires several trips. You'll encounter dramatic blufftop views and a variety of natural environments, from beaches and sea cliffs to woods and meadows. Wildlife thrives here: for several days during the summer of 1981, a lost mountain lion (dubbed "D. B. Cougar") took refuge in the park's dense woods.

Setting out on foot from the parking lot at the south entrance, you'll cross the wide South Meadow, past blackberry brambles, to sandy bluffs. People who thrill at an unrestricted view of Puget Sound and the Olympic Mountains will find this lofty site ideal for a picnic. You can even see the tip of Mount Rainier to the southeast. Children often play hide-and-seek among the sand dunes and shrubs.

If you prefer a long, driftwood-strewn beach complete with a historic lighthouse and teeming tide pools, follow the trail from the bluffs down to South Beach. You can visit West Point Lighthouse, built in 1881, weekends and holidays from 1:00 to 4:00 P.M. For information, call 282-9130. At low tide, a sandspit extending from the beach into Puget Sound becomes hikeable.

The full-time naturalists at the visitor center, located at the east entrance to the park (at West Government Way and 36th Avenue West), regularly provide pamphlets, lectures, and guided tours of the trails and beaches. Favorites for family exploring are the gentle Wolf Tree Interpretative Trail, a ½-mile, self-guided trail through a forest of conifer and deciduous trees with signs explaining points of interest. The 2.8-mile Loop Trail encircles the center of the park.

The Daybreak Star Indian Cultural Center (open weekdays 8:30 A.M. to 5:00 P.M. and weekends 10:00 A.M. to 5:00 P.M.), offers a place for families to view Native American art and artifacts, and observe or take part in heritage activities. Call 285-4425 to check the current schedule of events.

FOSTER ISLAND

A small, wooded island in the city with a view north to Union Bay.

Trail begins at the Museum of History and Industry's parking lot.

Located just north of Hwy 520 and the Washington Park Arboretum. From Hwy 520, take the Montlake Boulevard exit. The Museum of History and Industry is located north of the exit, two blocks east of Montlake Boulevard at 2700 24th Avenue East. The Washington Park Arboretum Waterfront Trail begins in the northeast corner of the Museum of History and Industry's parking lot.

Hours: Daily, dawn to dusk.
No tables, barbecues, water, or restrooms.
Pets, biking and jogging prohibited on the trail.
Bus routes: 25, 43, 48, 68, 77, 243

Follow a marshland trail through towering grasses and purple loosestrife to a wooded island. From Foster Island's grassy clearing you can watch the boats in Lake Washington and capture a view of the University of Washington across Union Bay.

The Waterfront Trail traverses the largest wetlands left in Seattle. These marshlands provide a sanctuary for abundant bird life, including nearly a dozen species of wintering ducks. Great blue heron and red-winged blackbirds are often seen here. The one-mile round-trip nature trail to Foster Island starts at the Museum of History and Industry's parking lot and meanders over bridges and on floating walkways along open water and through the wetland's lush foliage. Several side trails branching from the main pathway lead to view platforms. Benches placed frequently along the trail provide a place to rest and pause for a closer look at the plant and animal life. To learn more about the area, an interpretive pamphlet that corresponds to the 27 signs posted along the trail is available at the trailhead or at the Arboretum Visitor Center.

Foster Island is rarely very crowded. Spread a blanket in the sun on the island's grassy bank for a picnic lunch. There, you have a front-row seat for the parade of boats passing through the Montlake Cut. Two benches are set among the trees.

After your picnic, you can either continue south along the trail to reach the Washington Park Arboretum or return to the Museum of History and Industry.

The Lake Washington Ship Canal Waterside Trail, a 1,200-foot path along the south shore of the Montlake Cut, joins the Waterfront Trail at the museum parking lot. The ship canal trail, landscaped by the Army Corps of Engineers and the Seattle Garden Club, ends at West Montlake Park. This waterside park, shaded by poplar trees, is an excellent place to view the sunset.

The marshy channels north of the Washington Park Arboretum invite exploration by canoe. Canoe rentals are available for $3.50 per hour at the University of Washington Waterfront Activities Center, located behind Husky Stadium, across the water from Foster Island.

GRAND CENTRAL ARCADE

A grand lobby in the historic Pioneer Square district.

214 First Avenue South, Seattle.

Located in the heart of Seattle's historic Pioneer Square district. Take the James Street exit from I-5. Head west on James Street down the hill to First Avenue. Turn south (left) onto First Avenue and drive two blocks.

Hours: Weekdays, 7:00 A.M. to 6:00 P.M.; weekends, 9:00 A.M. to 5:00 P.M.
Tables, water, and restrooms are available. No barbecues.
Bus routes: 15, 18, 91

For those days when it is too damp to picnic outside, board the Waterfront Trolley at its northern terminus and head south to the Grand Central Arcade in Pioneer Square. (See Waterfront Streetcar, page 223.) The trolley stops at Occidental Park, just outside the entrance to the arcade. In the arcade, you can purchase hot drinks and custom-made sandwiches from the Grand Central Baking Company and enjoy them picnic-style in an elegant, old, heavy-beamed lobby surrounded by shops.

The arcade stands on the site of Seattle's first opera house, destroyed in the Great Fire of 1889 that burned most of the city's core. A massive rebuilding took place, this time in brick. During the gold rush, the building was called the Grand Central and became one of the city's fancier hotels; though not all its history was as illustrious. For many years following Pioneer Square's decline in the 1930s, it was run as a flophouse. During the 1970s, the building was one of the first in the district to be restored, and its success helped rekindle public interest in revitalizing the rest of the Pioneer Square district. The building is now known as Grand Central on the Park.

Through the rear doors of the arcade's lobby, you can see Occidental Park, a cobblestone square surrounded by London plane trees. Wrought-iron benches, mounted police in period uniforms, and an occasional horse-drawn carriage enhance Pioneer Square's turn-of-the-century flavor. Four totem poles, replicas of Northwest Coast Indian totem poles carved by local artist Duane Pasco, stand at the north end of the park.

For a good historical introduction to Pioneer Square, visit the Klondike Museum, located just south of the arcade on Main Street. This indoor national park, together with its sister unit in Skagway, Alaska, interprets Seattle's role in the 1897 gold rush to Alaska and the Yukon Territory. The stampede began when the coastal steamer *Portland* arrived in Seattle in 1897 and unloaded two tons of gold. More gold seekers left from Seattle than from any other city. First Avenue was alive with eager prospectors anxious to try their luck. Before embarking on their quest, they could practice their panning and dogsledding techniques at schools, such as the Yukon Mining School that was once on Second Avenue.

Galleries, antique stores, restaurants, and cafes are within strolling distance. One of Seattle's most popular bookstores, the Elliott Bay Book Company at First Avenue and Main Street, draws loyal customers with its well-stocked shelves, knowledgeable staff, long hours, basement deli, and frequent author readings.

MADRONA PARK

A park on Lake Washington with a view of Mount Rainier.

853 Lake Washington
Boulevard, Seattle.
684-4081

Located on the western shore
of Lake Washington between
the Hwy 520 and I-90 bridges.
Follow Lake Washington
Boulevard south from the
Arboretum until you see
the Madrona Dance Studio
building.

Hours: Daily, dawn to dusk.
Tables, barbecues, water, and
    restrooms are available.
Bus route: 2

Madrona Park is one of the prime
spots along Lake Washington's
shore. This wide, grassy waterfront strip is shaded by tall trees
(even a few madrona trees) and
includes a swimming beach, picnic
shelter, a dance studio, and a
popular concession stand that sells
barbecued chicken and ribs.

Sandy, bulkheaded beaches are
located in the park's south end,
with lifeguards on duty during the
summer. Picnic tables can be
found to the north near the concession stand. The park is an ex-
cellent place to watch the frequent summer sailing regattas launched
by the Corinthian Yacht Club from their Leschi clubhouse.

The upper park, a naturalized hillside across the street, was once the
pathway for a trolley track to the beach. Hoping to finalize lucrative
real estate deals, Seattle Electric Company added a hotel, boathouse, swings, and picnic shelters to the streetcar terminus. The city
bought the property in 1908 to use as a public beach. The brick
bathhouse was built in 1928. In 1971, the Madrona Dance Studio
took over use of the building. Today, Spectrum Dance Theatre is the
artistic company in residence, offering dance lessons and workshops.

MYRTLE EDWARDS PARK

A long neck of green stretching north from Pier 70 on Elliott Bay.

Alaskan Way between West Bay and West Thomas streets, north of downtown Seattle.
684-4081

The northern stretch of downtown waterfront. From I-5, take the Mercer Street exit. Turn right (north) on Fairview Avenue North and immediately left onto Valley Street. Keep left as the street curves around the south end of Lake Union and becomes Broad Street. Continue west to the water. Pier 70 lies at the foot of Broad Street. The park begins just north of the parking lot at Pier 70.

Hours: Daily, dawn to dusk.
Water and restrooms are
    available. No tables or
    barbecues.
Bus routes: 19, 24, 33

A popular noontime lunch spot for office workers, Myrtle Edwards Park is a long, sunny stretch of grass and pathways. Benches facing brisk sea breezes command water-level views of excursion and freighter traffic on Puget Sound and dramatic bay-and-sky views. To the south lies the Seattle cityscape.

There is one small sandy beach in Myrtle Edwards Park that is big enough to spread a blanket. Otherwise, claim one of the benches along the pathways. There are no tables. Less than two miles long, the Elliott Bay Bikeway begins in Myrtle Edwards Park and follows the shoreline through Elliott Bay Park, and past the loading docks for the grain terminals, to Smith Cove Park at Pier 91. This open, exposed arm of green is a favorite route for lunchtime joggers.

In 1979, the city commissioned artist Michael Heizer to chisel the park's now famous modern sculpture, *Adjacent, Against, Upon.*

A controversial addition to the landscape at that time, the work shows three quarried boulders positioned next to, against, and on top of three poured concrete bases. The sculpture alone is worth a visit to the park.

Just south of the park, the Waterfront Streetcar begins its 20-minute ride along the waterfront to Pioneer Square and the International District.

PARSONS GARDENS

A tree-enclosed garden.

Seventh West and West Highland Drive, Seattle. 684-4081

Located on the southwest edge of Queen Anne Hill. Take the Mercer Street exit from I-5 and drive west. At Queen Anne Avenue North, turn north up the hill to West Highland Drive and turn west.

Hours: Daily, 8:00 A.M. to 9:00 P.M.
Benches are available.
  No tables, barbecues, water, or restrooms.
Bus routes: 2, 13

Tucked in a Queen Anne neighborhood of gracious old homes and narrow winding streets, Parsons Gardens is a fairy-tale enclosure bordered by blooming trees and shrubs. The park is edged on three sides by quiet residential streets, but the moment you enter one of its gates, you step into your own secret garden. Privacy and seclusion are created by lush overhanging foliage surrounding a green lawn and rose gardens. A paved path circles the perimeter of the garden, under flowering cherry trees and among perennial flower beds. Stepping-stones lead to a latticed shelter that shades two English garden benches where you can spread your picnic.

Once the garden of the Reginald H. Parsons family, it was given to the city by the Parsons children in memory of their parents and opened to the public in 1956. The garden is often reserved for weddings. If one is planned for the day you visit, a sign will be posted on the gate.

Across the street from Parsons Gardens is Marshall Viewpoint, a tiny wedge of hillside with a magnificent view of Puget Sound, the Olympics, and Elliott Bay. Three benches, a grassy slope, and a bit of shade comprise the overlook, from which you can capture dramatic sunset views. Prominent Northwest artists such as Victor Steinbrueck and Morris Graves have traced figurative outlines into the cement walkway.

SEATTLE UNIVERSITY

A restful, urban campus on Capitol Hill.

Broadway at Madison, Seattle.
296-6464

Located on the east side of
Broadway Avenue across from
Swedish Hospital. Take the
James Street exit from I-5 and
drive east on James to 12th
Avenue. Turn north on 12th
Avenue to the Seattle University
visitor parking lot on the west
(left) side of the street.

Hours: Daily, 8:00 A.M. to dusk.
Tables, barbecues, restrooms,
    and water are available.
Fees: $1.00 for parking
Bus routes: 9, 11

Step onto the grounds of Seattle
University and you'll realize you
have entered an urban oasis. This
campus is filled with blossoms in
the spring and offers several quiet
refuges.

Four sites here serve as unex-
pected havens from the city and
are especially inviting for picnics:
a sunny plaza with a fountain; a
sheltered pocket park; a protected
expanse of lawn near a grotto; and
an enclosed Japanese garden with
a miniature waterfall and pool.

The large, open plaza up the hill
from the visitor parking lot resembles a Zen garden, where form and
sound and the elements of nature interact. In the middle of the
square, George Tsutakawa's *Centennial Fountain* casts a spray of water
several feet skyward before drops fall to a shallow pool at its base.
A temple bell and flowering cherry trees add further touches of
Japan. You can spread a picnic on the terraced slopes or sit on one
of the flat boulders or steps.

On the other side of the Pigott Building north of the plaza, you'll find
an enclosed pocket park with tables, barbecues, and a mini-fountain

with a three-dimensional likeness of Chief Seattle's face. In addition to being a choice spot to enjoy a quiet lunch for two, the garden is also a bird sanctuary.

Look for a stretch of lawn and a grotto hidden behind the Administration Building on the far northwest corner of the campus. Cherry trees line the walk and a small stone grotto to the Virgin Mary stands in a far corner, near a bench.

South of James Street and the main part of the university and just north of Campion Hall, you'll find a secluded, peaceful Japanese garden designed by Fujitaro Kubota. He was a friend of the former Jesuit gardener on campus, Father Raymond Nichols (affectionately known as "Father Greengrass"), and they often worked together in the various campus gardens. The Japanese garden was considered by Kubota to be his best work on campus. Enter through an opening in the picket fence near the parking lot. Inside, you will find a small waterfall, a pond, and picnic tables on a stone patio.

SMITH COVE PARK

A tiny, green waterfront viewspot on an earth-filled pier.

Pier 91, Seattle.
684-4081

Located at the southern base of Magnolia Bluff on the Seattle waterfront. From Elliott Avenue, take West Dravus Street to Thorndyke Avenue West. Turn south (left) on Thorndyke and drive to 24th Avenue West. A sign on the left marks the entrance to the park.

Hours: Daily, 8:00 A.M. to dusk.
Tables are available. No
   barbecues or water. One
   portable toilet at end of the
   parking lot.
Bus routes: 19, 24, 33

Few people have discovered what lies at the end of the road to Pier 91. Follow the 0.7-mile lane that winds past warehouses and hundreds of parked imported cars to this tiny park with one of the city's most striking water views. Just west of the great earth-filled piers, the park itself is part of the working harbor's landscape. Huge barges are moored at the adjacent pier; container ships and ferries ply the waters of the bay. You'll have a panoramic view south and west that takes in the downtown skyline, West Seattle, and the Olympic Mountains.

From the parking lot, a concrete walkway along a bouldered bulkhead leads to a small lawn. Six picnic tables and six benches are spaced along the slender stretch of parkland. At low tide, you can scramble over the boulders to a sandy beach for more secluded picnicking.

Bicyclists can easily reach Smith Cove Park via the Elliott Bay Bikeway, which connects Myrtle Edwards Park to the Discovery Park loop.

A historical plaque marks the history of Pier 91. Early shipping on this part of the harbor began in 1891, when coal was loaded from railroad cars onto steam and sailing ships berthed at the Northern Pacific Coal Bunker Pier. At the turn of the century, Piers 88 and 89 were completed, linking the Transcontinental Railroad to the Orient. Large ships, loaded with precious silk, docked at Smith Cove every three weeks. The silk then traveled by high-speed train to the New York garment market. The first silk train left Seattle in 1909 and the last one around 1933. The speed record was set in 1924, when 2,280 bales of silk arrived in New York a short 12 days, 1 hour, and 15 minutes after leaving port in Yokohama, Japan.

In 1912, the Port of Seattle purchased the tideflats now known as Piers 90 and 91 and began construction of the earth-filled piers, which were the largest in the world at their completion in 1921. The Port operated these piers until 1962, then sold them to the U.S. Navy for service during the Vietnam War. In 1975, the Port repurchased the piers and operates them today.

UNION SQUARE PLAZA

A sunny trilevel open-air courtyard with a waterfall and flowers.

Sixth Avenue between
University and Union streets,
Seattle.
628-5050

Located in downtown Seattle,
just west and south of the
Washington State Convention
and Trade Center. Take the
Union Street (southbound) or
Seneca Street (northbound)
exits from I-5. Union Square
Plaza is located just off the
Union Street exit. From the
Seneca Street exit, turn north
onto Sixth Avenue to Union
Street.

Hours: Daily, 8:00 A.M. to
   10:00 P.M.
Tables are available. No
   barbecues or water.
   Restrooms are in the Two
   Union Square building.
Bus routes: 2, 3, 4, 7, 11, 14, 20

In the summer at Union Square
Plaza, you can combine lunch in
an elegant courtyard with a noontime concert. Every Thursday at
noon from June to September, a
different musical ensemble gathers to play here, attracting an
appreciative audience of office
workers and accidental concert-
goers who wander onto the plaza
from the Convention Center
next door.

If you enter from the upper level
from Sixth and University, you
can gaze down over the courtyard
and choose your spot to picnic.
You can find a vacant table, sit on
a low step or wall, or claim one of
the canvas cushions brought out
by the local merchants whenever
a summer concert is scheduled.
If you enter from the lower level
at Sixth and Union, your eye will be drawn to the dramatic waterfall
that cascades three stories through the courtyard. The water is
turned off during the concerts.

Columns, fountains, carved images, and colorful flowers spilling over ledges suggest the atmosphere of an ancient Roman villa. Protected balconies and tables with umbrellas (not all tables belong to a restaurant) look down three levels to the central courtyard.

You can purchase picnic fare from several take-out restaurants bordering the plaza. In addition to boutiques, a cafe, a deli, a grill, and an espresso bar opened their doors when the towering office building was completed in 1990.

Walk up the stairs on the north side of the plaza to enter Freeway Park, a multitiered strip of grass, trees, and water set above the freeway and amid towering downtown buildings. Follow the winding paths and stairways through a massive, labyrinthine concrete canyon with a thundering waterfall that masks the surrounding traffic. Tall deciduous trees, and colorful flowers and plantings in giant cement boxes create such an impressive display of green that it's difficult to believe you're above eight lanes of traffic.

Even if you don't work in the area, the Union Square Plaza is easy to get to by bus or on foot from the monorail station, or from the Convention Place, Westlake, or University Street underground bus tunnel stations.

WASHINGTON PARK ARBORETUM

Wooded parkland and research gardens bordered by Lake Washington.

2300 Arboretum Drive East,
Seattle.
543-8800 (Visitor Center)

Located south of the University
of Washington across the ship
canal. From Hwy 520
(westbound), take the Lake
Washington Boulevard exit.
From Hwy 520 (eastbound),
take the Montlake Boulevard
exit and cross Montlake
Boulevard at the light straight
onto Lake Washington
Boulevard. Lake Washington
Boulevard runs through the
center of the Arboretum.

Hours: Arboretum: Daily,
    8:00 A.M. to sunset.
Visitor Center: Weekdays,
    10:00 A.M. to 3:45 P.M.;
    weekends, 12:00 P.M. to
    3:45 P.M.
Japanese Garden: Open daily,
    March through November,
    at 10:00 A.M. Closing times
    vary by season. Closed
    December through
    February. $1.50 entrance
    fee to Japanese Garden.

The Arboretum is a special place
in any season, but the bloom and
color of spring and fall are particularly magical. A beautiful
wooded parkland with lush gardens and more than 5,500 native
and exotic plantings, this serene
setting is a delightful spot for a
romantic picnic.

Pathways weave through formal
garden settings, groves of magno-
lias and maples, open grassy areas,
and wild marshland. Rhododendrons and azaleas of astonishing
hues burst into brilliance in spring.
The main walking path is Azalea
Way, which begins at the visitor
center on Arboretum Drive at the
north end of the park, and runs
through the center of the park
to end at the Japanese Garden.
Several pathways branch off
Azalea Way to specialized planting areas, such as the conifer
meadow, winter garden, and
rhododendron glen. Pick any spot

Tables, barbecues, water, and restrooms are available.

Bus routes: 11, 43, 48, 49. Several routes cross the Evergreen Point Floating Bridge and stop at the Montlake off-ramp shelter three blocks north of the Arboretum.

that suits your mood and spread your blanket.

Although picnics are not permitted there, the Japanese Garden, located at the south end of the Arboretum off Lake Washington Boulevard East, deserves a special visit. This secluded garden, built in 1960, is a composition of graceful bridges, stone lanterns, Japanese maples, a 12-tiered pagoda, and a waterfall cascading down to a carp-filled pool — the whole design of which urges tranquil reflection. An authentic tea house, rebuilt after a fire destroyed the original, is the setting for *Chado* (the Way of Tea) demonstrations. Call ahead for information at 324-1483.

The visitor center provides information on the park, offers monthly naturalist-led tours of the gardens, and has horticultural displays and a gift shop. The Arboretum Foundation's annual plant sales are very popular and often the only source for obtaining disappearing Northwest species.

WASHINGTON STATE FERRY SYSTEM

A picnic while crossing Puget Sound.

Colman Dock, Pier 52, Seattle. 464-6400 for ferry information, including schedules.

Located at Pier 52 on Alaskan Way. From I-5, take the James Street exit. Turn west on Columbia Street and continue down the hill to the waterfront. Turn north on Alaskan Way. Parking is available at several lots located on Western Avenue, one block east of Alaskan Way.

Hours: Daily. Call for schedule.
Tables, water, and restrooms
   are available. No barbecues.
Fee: $3.30 round-trip to
   Bremerton (foot passengers);
   $3.30 round-trip to
   Bainbridge (foot passengers)
Bus routes: 12, 15, 18 (on
   1st Avenue), and 305

Rain or shine, a ferry ride conjures the romance and adventure of a cruise. The Washington State Ferry System makes a brief getaway a whole lot easier (and cheaper) than booking passage on a cruise ship. On clear days, Puget Sound's natural beauty is shown to full advantage. Ferry rides on wet, gray days can be just as intriguing and fun. Walk on the Bremerton ferry from Colman Dock (Pier 52) in downtown Seattle for your picnic on Puget Sound.

The Bremerton ferry is the longer of the two ferry runs that operate from Colman Dock. The ride lasts about an hour each way, with stunning island, water, mountain, and city views. If it is a clear day, you can picnic on the top deck in the sun and salt breeze. If the cold drives you inside, plenty of tables and booths can usually be found. Bring your own picnic fare to avoid the long lines at the on-board food concession. The ferries are crowded during holidays and commuter hours; try to plan your trip around peak travel times.

Once you arrive at the First Street Dock in Bremerton, located one block down the hill from town, foot passengers have a choice of several excursions.

The Bremerton Naval Museum (130 Washington Avenue) has exhibits devoted to the naval history of the area, including the heroism during World War II of the men aboard the USS *Enterprise*. (In May 1991, the Vietnam-era destroyer, USS *Turner Joy*, will be berthed just north of the ferry terminal and open for tours.)

For further exploring, Illahee State Park in East Bremerton is a beautiful wooded bluff 250 feet above Port Orchard Bay. At low tide, you can climb down the steep, switchback trail to walk along a sandy beach. You can get to the park from the ferry terminal by catching a Kitsap transit bus (#29 Trenton Avenue). Look for the bus-loading sign painted on the street. The buses leave the ferry terminal on the hour from 8:00 A.M. to 6:00 P.M. and travel to a stop at Trenton Avenue and Sylvan Way, a 15-minute walk from the park. Call Kitsap Transit System at 373-2877 for more information.

Also within walking or biking distance is the passenger-only ferry from Bremerton across Sinclair Inlet to Port Orchard, a small, picturesque town known for its antique shops and two small historical museums. From the Port Orchard ferry, you will have a good look at the activity in the naval shipyard. The ferry leaves every 30 minutes from a well-marked pier just north of the Washington State Ferry dock and costs 70 cents each way for adults, 45 cents each way for children and bicycles.

WATERFALL GARDEN

An enclosed urban retreat with a cascading wall of water.

Corner of Second Avenue South and South Main Street, Seattle. 624-6096

Located in Pioneer Square. From I-5, take the James Street exit. Follow James Street to Second Avenue, turn south and drive for three blocks.

Hours: Daily, 10:00 A.M. to 5:00 P.M. Summer months: daily, 10:00 A.M. to 8:00 P.M. Tables are available. No barbecues, water, or restrooms. Restrooms are in nearby shops.
Bus routes: 39, 136, 137, and several other routes along Second Avenue.

Ideally, the purpose of a lunch break is to restore, refresh, and renew. These requirements are not always easily satisfied in the urban bustle of downtown Seattle. There exists, however, a secret refuge not far from the Kingdome and the world of commerce, hidden behind the brick walls at Second Avenue and South Main Street.

Water tumbles from a 22-foot-high wall and washes away the sounds of the city; on a bright day, sunlight plays on leaves and flowers. The overall effect is like walking by a rushing mountain stream.

Waterfall Garden was designed to make the most of the small space. An upper level, covered by an arched roof, is ringed by a small stream of water. Open to the sky, the lower level is a place for sitting in the sun. Sixteen white garden tables with chairs and several benches are spaced on both levels. During summer evenings, lights illuminate the interior of the garden, and in winter, heating elements warm the upper-level tables. A concession stand with a limited snack menu operates in one corner of the park.

The garden was opened in 1978 as a gift of the Annie E. Casey Foundation to honor men and women of the United Parcel Service. The company was started in 1907 in a basement office underneath the garden site. The foundation now operates the park and snack bar.

Waterfall Garden is located just steps away from the concentration of art galleries in Pioneer Square. It's a perfect place for a summer evening picnic supper before attending the Gallery Walk, when galleries open their doors during evening hours to display new exhibits. The walk takes place the first Thursday of each month, but check the arts section of the Seattle newspapers to make sure, as there are exceptions.

WATERFRONT STREETCAR

A moveable feast through three downtown districts.

Northern station is located at Pier 70. Southern terminus is located at Fifth Avenue and Jackson. Several stops along Alaskan Way and Main Street. 447-4800

To get to the northern terminus, take the Mercer Street exit from I-5. Turn right (north) on Fairview Avenue North and immediately left onto Valley Street. Keep left as the street curves around the south end of Lake Union and becomes Broad Street. Pier 70 lies at the foot of Broad Street.

Hours: Daily, October through February, 7:10 A.M. to 6:00 P.M.; extended hours during the summer.
Fare: 55 cents off-peak commuter hours; 75 cents during peak hours.
No tables, barbecues, restrooms or water.
Handicapped access to trolley.
Bus routes: 15, 18
    (on First Avenue)

The Waterfront Streetcar is a colorful and leisurely way for tourists and residents alike to get around the downtown waterfront. From the northern end of the run at Myrtle Edwards Park (Pier 70), the trolley travels south along Alaskan Way below Pike Place Market, then east through Pioneer Square, to its new station at Fifth Avenue and Jackson Street in the International District. Along the way, you can, if you plan your menu accordingly, enjoy a mobile picnic on the wood and leather benches of the antique trolleys while passing through three distinct Seattle neighborhoods. You won't be alone: office and shop workers often picnic on the trolley during a lunch break. Fish 'n' chips and other take-out provisions are plentiful along the streetcar's route.

The two-mile ride takes about 20 minutes each way, with a

20-minute wait at either end. This rather slow pace allows you time to eat lunch, enjoy the surroundings, and observe the waterfront activity. You might wish to get off and explore a bit. Though Seattle's working harbor has moved south, this tourist-oriented stretch of downtown waterfront is still fun for a taste of salt air, for people watching, maybe for a browse through a curio shop. Definitely worth visiting is the Seattle Aquarium (625-4537) at Pier 59. The trolley stops directly in front of the aquarium.

If you do want to get out at any of the nine stops along the route, ask for a transfer as you leave the car. You may then reboard within 90 minutes at no additional cost.

South of the ferry terminal (Pier 52), the trolley turns west on South Main Street to the historic Pioneer Square district. Here, nearly 140 years ago on what was originally a mudflat and a steep, wooded ridge, Seattle was founded. Now the district is the center of the city's fine arts scene, with numerous galleries; you'll also find crafts shops, bookstores, antique shops, taverns, and many restaurants.

The southern terminus of the trolley is the brightly painted station in the International District. In this neighborhood, Chinese, Japanese, Filipino, Korean, and Southeast Asian communities have retained their cultural and linguistic identities and created a thriving district where people live and work. Scores of restaurants, wonderful small ethnic groceries, Chinese herbalists, the huge Uwajimaya emporium (519 Sixth Avenue South), and Wing Luke Asian Museum (407 Seventh Avenue South) are all within walking distance. Just across the street from the trolley station, the Metro underground bus tunnel provides easy access uptown.

CARL S. ENGLISH, JR., BOTANICAL GARDEN

(AT HIRAM M. CHITTENDEN LOCKS)

*A shaded garden and terraced lawn with a prime view
of the boating activity at the Ballard locks.*

3015 NW 54th Street, Seattle.
783-7059

Located on the north side of
the ship canal locks in Ballard.
From I-5, take the North 85th
Street exit. Follow 85th Street
west approximately three miles
to 32nd Avenue NW. Turn
south and drive 1½ miles to
NW 54th Street and the
entrance to the locks.

Hours: Daily, 7:00 A.M. to
   9:00 P.M.
Visitor Center: Summer, daily,
   10:00 A.M. to 7:00 P.M.;
   other seasons, Thursday to
   Monday, 11:00 A.M. to
   5:00 P.M.
Water and restrooms are
   available. No tables or
   barbecues.
Bus routes: 17, 18, 43, 46, 62

The Hiram M. Chittenden
Locks is a popular place year-
round for watching boat traffic
between Seattle's lakes and
Puget Sound. When summer
sun draws most visitors to the
locks, you'll find a retreat away
from the crowds with a view
of the maritime activity on the
terraced lawn of the Carl S.
English, Jr., Botanical Garden,
just above the locks on the north
side of the ship canal. People
often don't wander from the
concrete walkways near the
locks to stop at the garden, so
you might even have it all to
yourself.

West of the walkway to the
locks, seven acres of exotic and
native plants create a lush set-
ting for a picnic. Carl S. English, Jr., spent more than 30 years
designing and developing the botanical garden. Through his diligence

unusual trees, such as the Chilean fire tree and dawn redwood, found their way into Northwest soil. The garden features more than 1,000 species of trees, flowers, and shrubs, with some, like the Chinese witch hazel and fragrant wintersweet, chosen specifically because they bloom in winter. Throughout the spring and summer, roses, tulips, flowering crab apple and cherry trees, rhododendrons, and azaleas color the garden. In the spirit of Carl English, botanists from other states still offer rare seeds to the garden's resident horticulturist.

The idea of connecting the city's freshwater lakes and Puget Sound arose as early as 1853. In 1911, the Army Corps of Engineers began construction of the locks, which opened in 1917, and operates them today. Because Puget Sound is anywhere from 6 to 26 feet lower than the ship canal, two locks allow passage of more than 100,000 military, commercial, and pleasure boats each year. Sunday evenings feature a spectacle of recreational boats—sailboats, schooners, cabin cruisers, and motorboats—as weekend skippers make their way home. Weekdays, the working boats and crews reveal a different aspect of waterfront life.

The visitor center at the locks has a slide show and working models of the locks; a brochure and plant list available there will guide you through the garden.

A fish ladder permits migrating salmon to pass by the locks on their way to Lake Union and Lake Washington and the rivers that feed the lakes. An underground viewing area located just south of the locks provides a closeup view of salmon, sea-run trout, and steelhead as they struggle up the ladder to their freshwater spawning grounds. Salmon return from June through November; peak sock-eye salmon runs can be seen in the ladder during July. Cutthroat trout appear in the ladder from August to February, with their peak run in November. Steelhead can be seen from December through March, reaching a peak in January.

CENTER FOR URBAN HORTICULTURE

A small enclosed garden of ornamental grasses and trees.

3501 NE 41st Street, Seattle.
685-8033

Located north of the University of Washington intramural fields on the corner of Union Bay Place NE and NE 41st Street. From I-5, take the NE 45th Street exit and drive east. At the bottom of the viaduct, veer left, continuing east on 45th Street. At the next traffic light, turn south (right) onto Union Bay Place NE.

Hours: Monday through Friday, 8:30 A.M. to 5:00 P.M.
Water and restrooms are available. No tables or barbecues.
Bus routes: 25, 30, 32, 75

A wide trellised gate at the Center for Urban Horticulture leads past border groves of black bamboo into McVay Courtyard, a small, sunken garden planted with a delightful variety of ornamental grasses and foliage. You can spread your picnic lunch on a low stucco wall that serves as both bench and table. The enclosed courtyard is open to the sky and sun, but because of the garden's small scale, it feels intimate.

The Center for Urban Horticulture was conceived to promote the study of plants in an urban setting. Affiliated with the University of Washington and the Arboretum, the center is the first and largest of its kind in the United States and offers popular workshops on the plants of the Northwest coastal region.

Just beyond the garden is the Elisabeth Miller Library, a nonlending reference library open to the public. The library provides several free book lists on topics that include winter gardening, drought gardening, gardening with wildlife, care of trees and shrubs, and exploring nature with children.

South of the center lies the Montlake Fill, one of Seattle's most active birding spots. This area has been designated a wildlife sanctuary and ecological study zone, and attracts migrating birds often not seen anywhere else in the city. Birders come hoping to spot a hooded merganser, a snowy owl, or a green-backed heron. Wahkiakum Lane, a wide dirt path, leads to the start of a trail that winds for about a mile through the fill's open grassland and around marsh and ponds, to end at Ravenna Creek and the University of Washington playing fields.

GAS WORKS PARK

*Once an industrial eyesore, now a peaceful lakeside park
with a striking view of downtown Seattle.*

North Northlake Way and
Meridian Avenue North, Seattle.
684-4081

Located on the north shore
of Lake Union, west of the
University of Washington.
From I-5, take the NE 45th
Street exit and head west. Turn
south (left) on Meridian Avenue
North and follow it until you
reach the park.

Hours: Daily, dawn to dusk.
Tables, barbecues, water, and
restrooms are available.
Bus route: 26

You can easily identify Gas Works
Park at the north end of Lake
Union by the hulking skeleton of
the old gas manufacturing plant
at the water's edge. Built in 1906,
the gasworks operated until 1956,
when it was abandoned. The city
bought the site in 1962 and
trucked in tons of dirt and sawdust
to produce topsoil for growing
grass over sludge and tar left by
the gasworks. Now there is little
hint of what was once an industrial
wasteland.

The cogs, wheels, and giant engines of the old gas plant at the east end of the park have been transformed into a covered play barn where children can safely climb on machinery and investigate the workings. A large sheltered picnic area adjacent to the play barn has enough tables and barbecues for a family reunion. (Call 684-4801 to reserve a space.) Follow the waterfront promenade for exhilarating sky and water views.

The windswept 60-foot grassy knoll west of the play barn attracts kite flyers of all ages. A giant sundial at the top of the hill will show the time using your own shadow when you stand on the correct date marked in the center of the dial. Created by a local artist, the sundial's design incorporates objects found and collected from all over the world.

Gas Works Park is also host to a huge Fourth of July celebration when the Seattle Symphony accompanies a dramatic fireworks display over Lake Union. You must arrive early in the day in order to claim a picnic spot for this event.

MERIDIAN PARK

*An enclosed, wide lawn with gardens behind a grand,
turn-of-the-century building.*

Meridian Avenue North and
North 50th Street, Seattle.
684-4081

Located in the Wallingford
district. From I-5, take the
NE 50th Street exit and drive
west. Turn south (left) on
Meridian Avenue North and
park on the street.

Hours: Daily, dawn to dusk.
Tables, barbecues, water, and
restrooms are available.
Bus route: 16

Enter Meridian Park through a
stone archway and unusual winding path at the corner of Meridian Avenue North and North 50th
Street. This wonderful entry
opens to an expansive lawn
shaded by gnarled trees, a playground with slides and swings,
and cultivated gardens. The Good
Shepherd Center, a graceful, turn-
of-the-century building of brick
and stone, dominates the park's
east end. Thick hedges surround
the park and block busy streets
from view; the overall effect is romantic and inviting.

The western half of the park, with the flat, open grounds and
playground, is maintained by the Seattle Parks Department. The
eastern half, maintained by the Good Shepherd Center staff, has a
more formal, English garden look.

The Good Shepherd Center was built in 1905 and designed by
C. Alfred Breitung, the Austrian-born designer of Holy Names
Academy for girls on Capitol Hill. The Home of the Good Shepherd
operated over the years in different capacities—as a school, an
orphanage, and a home for "waywards." The grounds narrowly

escaped being converted into a shopping mall before the community and the city came to the site's rescue in the early 1970s. Several civic and arts organizations now have offices at the center, among them the Pacific Northwest Ballet.

The gazebo and covered picnic area in the center of the grounds is adjacent to Seattle Tilth's demonstration gardens. Espaliered fruit trees, curving garden paths, and a children's garden, in what was once a swimming pool, create a lovely picnic setting.

Seattle Tilth (633-0451) has made its home at the south end of the Good Shepherd Center since 1978. The organization provides information on sustainable urban agriculture. In addition to touring its demonstration gardens, you can consult its library and experts, learn about composting and earthworm farms, and attend its annual edible plant sale. Next to Tilth's gardens, Seattle P-patch gardeners harvest their bounty.

NATIONAL OCEANIC AND ATMOSPHERIC ADMINISTRATION (NOAA) GROUNDS

Public artworks along a quiet shoreline walk.

7600 Sand Point Way NE, Seattle.
526-6385

Located on NOAA's regional center grounds on Lake Washington. From I-5, take the NE 65th Street exit. Drive east on NE 65th Street to Sand Point Way NE. Turn north. Enter the NOAA gate and park near Lot 1.

Hours: Daily, 6:00 A.M. to 7:00 P.M.
Tables are located behind the NOAA cafeteria (open to the public); water and restrooms are available in the NOAA buildings. No barbecues.
Bus routes: 41, 74, 75

Once behind the open steel gate, past huge government warehouses, and beyond the parking lots, you will discover a peaceful stretch of shoreline. NOAA opened its regional center here in 1982 and, in conjunction with the Seattle Arts Commission, created a unique series of artworks by five artists, arranged along a lakefront path. Set in the grassy, open terrain of a designated wildlife enhancement area, these "working" pieces are shaped by their natural surroundings.

Begin your walk at the west end of Building 1, where you will find the first in the series, *Knoll for NOAA*, by Martin Puryear. Continue down the slope behind the building to join the shoreline walk. The next work, *Viewpoint*, by Scott Burton, is a meditative spot for a picnic set in a grove of trees along the water. Sit on one of the eight benches chiseled from granite and take in superb views of the north end of Lake Washington.

The exposed shoreline catches the breezes off the lake, which are captured in haunting tones in the *Sound Garden*, by artist Douglas Hollis. Tuned pipe organs supported on metal towers create an eerie music with every breath of wind. Listen to the change in tone and intensity as you walk along the path that weaves through the towers. You can even feel the vibrations of sound emitted by the giant pipes. Benches placed within the "garden" invite you to stop and listen to the wonderful and mysterious sounds accompanied by gorgeous water views.

Other works on the walk include two unusual bridges with a Moby Dick theme by Siah Armajani; and *Berth Haven*, a wood-and-steel dock, by George Trakas. If you wish to continue your stroll, the shoreline walk connects the NOAA grounds to the north end of Magnuson Park. This large, family-oriented park on Lake Washington has a popular swimming beach, an elaborate play area, sports fields, and bicycle and walking paths, in addition to delightful lake views. A small gate connecting the NOAA grounds and Magnuson Park opens daily at 6:30 A.M. and closes at 7:00 P.M.

SUNSET HILL PARK

A small wayside park above Shilshole Marina.

NW 75th Street and 34th
Avenue NW, Seattle.
684-4081

Located in west Ballard. From
I-5, take the North 85th Street
exit. Drive west approximately
3½ miles to 32nd Avenue NW
and turn south (left). At NW
75th Street, turn west (right).
The park is straight ahead.

Hours: Daily, dawn to dusk.
Tables and benches are
available. No water,
barbecues, or restrooms.
Bus route: 17

Nothing elaborate—just a patch
of green and a tiny rose garden
in a quiet Ballard neighborhood,
but Sunset Hill Park commands
one of Seattle's most impressive
water views. Picnic here for spectacular sunset vistas against the
backdrop of the jagged Olympics
and smooth waters of Puget
Sound. The viewpoint, dedicated
to the Seattle fishing fleet and to
those who have lost their lives at
sea, sits on a ridge overlooking
Shilshole Bay Marina. It's a quiet
place for sea gazing and for
watching the boats glide in and out of the marina.

Three benches and a lone picnic table are rarely occupied. The park
is open to the street and offers no privacy, but all of your attention
will be focused on the view west, anyway. The best picnic spot is the
bench screened by the roses.

Parking on the street next to the park is prohibited between 10:00 P.M.
and 6:00 A.M.

UNIVERSITY OF WASHINGTON

Three picnic spots in a lovely campus setting: a historic medicinal herb garden, a small grove with English park benches, and the Quadrangle lawn under falling cherry blossoms.

Main entrance: NE 45th Street and 17th Avenue NE, Seattle. 543-2100

Located in northeast Seattle. From I-5, take the NE 45th Street exit and drive east, about one mile. Obtain a campus map at the information center located at the entrance.

Benches, water, and restrooms are available. No barbecues. Fees: Parking is available for $4.00.

Bus routes: 43, 48, 71, 72, 73, 74

Lawns and gardens, a wealth of trees, elegant and diverse architecture, open space and mountain vistas—all combine to make the University of Washington in Seattle an exceptionally beautiful urban campus. In addition to many choice picnic spots, you will find two museums to explore, a huge bookstore near campus for browsing, a basement coffeehouse for refreshments, and lovely grounds for strolling.

Three delightful places on campus for sharing a box lunch are: the Liberal Arts Quadrangle, Grieg Grove, and the Medicinal Herb Garden.

A spectacular blooming display takes place each spring on the Liberal Arts Quadrangle. Thirty large Yoshino cherry trees, their dark, gnarled wood set off by the delicate blossoms, release a dazzling carpet of pink every April. Spread your blanket on the lawn underneath the trees and examine the carved figures on the Gothic buildings bordering the quadrangle.

Grieg Grove, near the new Suzzallo Library addition at the center of the campus, is a quiet, enclosed garden. A large bronze bust of Norwegian composer Edvard Grieg from the Alaska-Yukon-Pacific Exposition, held at the University in 1909, identifies this spot. Shaded by Spanish chestnut and white birch trees, five English garden benches placed around the garden invite a picnic lunch.

Those who have an interest in cooking or plant lore will be drawn to the Medicinal Herb Garden, established in 1911. With more than 625 plants, shrubs, and herbs, it is a living museum and the largest garden of its type in the western hemisphere. Hidden behind tall border hedges, the garden seldom hosts more than one visitor at a time.

The herb garden encompasses two acres, and includes 125 different kinds of trees, many of them rare in Seattle. The beds, maintained entirely by volunteers, contain labeled plantings used for cooking, cosmetics, dyes, and medicinal purposes. During World War I, the garden produced critical supplies of belladonna, digitalis, and other plant drugs.

You can picnic on the small lawn or sit on the rustic benches and enjoy an herbal picnic. Enter the garden through two wooden columns across Stevens Way from the Botany Department greenhouses.

There is much to see and do on campus. The Henry Art Gallery, located on the southwest edge of campus, has a wide range of rotating exhibits and special events in addition to its permanent collection of 19th- and 20th-century American and European paintings, prints, and ceramics. At the north end of campus, the Burke

Memorial Washington State Museum is a natural history and anthropology museum with a fine collection of Northwest Coast Indian artifacts. Espresso and pastries can be purchased at the Boiserie coffeehouse, located in the basement of the Burke Museum. And if you would like to browse in one of the largest bookstores in the country, the University Book Store is just off campus at 4326 University Way NE.

Woodland Park Zoological Gardens and Rose Garden

Benches and picnic tables set among open animal habitats.

5500 Phinney Avenue North, Seattle.
684-4800

Located west of Aurora Avenue (Hwy 99), southwest of Green Lake. From I-5, take the NE 50th Street exit and drive west. The south entrance of the zoo is located at North 50th and Fremont Avenue North.

Hours: March to October, weekdays, 10:00 A.M. to 6:00 P.M.; weekends, 8:30 A.M. to 6:00 P.M.; November to February, daily, 10:00 A.M. to 4:00 P.M. The zoo is open every day of the year, including holidays.
Tables, water, and restrooms are available. No barbecues.
Fees: $4.00 for adults; $2.00 seniors and youths; children under 6 free. Thursdays are free. Parking lot is $1.00. Wheelchairs and strollers for rent at the gift shop near the zoo's south entrance.
Bus route: 5

Woodland Park Zoo is not for children only. Adults, too, will delight in strolling the walkways that turn and twist to reveal one animal surprise after another. Once a traditional zoo with animals caged behind bars, much of Woodland Park Zoo has been transformed into an attractive park in which animals roam in natural settings designed to duplicate their habitats in the wild. Enhanced with imaginative public-art pieces, winding paths, and interesting exhibits, Woodland Park Zoo makes a wonderful site for a family picnic and outing.

Picnic spots are varied. The zoo is laid out in such a way that you can explore one part of the zoo and return another day for a different view (and another picnic). You can choose among an African savannah, the thick woods of an Asian elephant forest, a family farm with hatching chicks, and an open meadow on the zoo's north end (near the pony rides) where children can run freely. Most exhibits have nearby benches for resting, picnicking, or people (and animal) watching. Tables are situated near the north and south entrances for easy access to the picnic supplies in your car. An ideal spot is the table located just next to the Asian elephant forest. And if your group is more than four, try to claim the row of tables shaded by large trees on the lawn just outside the entrance to the family farm.

Concession stands in several locations sell hot dogs, drinks, and other snack items. The gift shop at the south entrance has strollers and wheelchairs available for rent. The zoo also hosts concerts, tours, lectures, and classes. Call for information.

For a change in mood and setting, the rose garden just outside the zoo's south gate inspires a more leisurely pace. Hidden behind tall hedges and an iron gate, this garden has a manicured lawn surrounding more than 190 varieties of roses. The elegant garden was first created by Guy Phinney in the 1890s as part of his Woodland Park estate.

The rich fragrance and palette of the roses provide the perfect atmosphere for a romantic tea or lunch. The roses are part of a symmetrical grid that includes benches, ponds, and sculpted trees. During the blooming period, from late May through August, the garden is so well tended that there are few petals on the ground.

The garden is open until dusk each day.

EMMA SCHMITZ MEMORIAL OVERLOOK AND ME-KWA-MOOKS PARK

A sea-level promenade and former hillside estate in West Seattle with a sweeping view of Puget Sound and the Olympics.

Beach Drive SW and
SW Oregon Street, Seattle.
684-4075

Located south of the Alki Point Lighthouse in West Seattle. Take the West Seattle exit from Hwy 99 or the Spokane Street exit from I-5. Follow the West Seattle freeway across the West Seattle bridge, and continue driving to the top of the hill. Keep west (right) onto SW Alaska Street and drive to 49th Avenue SW. Turn south (left) and drive two blocks to SW Hudson Street; turn west (right). Hudson becomes Jacobson Road. At Beach Drive SW, turn north (right) and drive two blocks to the overlook and park.

Hours: Daily, dawn to dusk.
Tables are available. No
  barbecues, water, or
  restrooms.
Bus route: 37

The view west from Emma Schmitz Memorial Overlook is unexcelled: a 240-degree sweep from Vashon Island to the south, past Blake Island, and north to the lighthouse at Alki Point. Five wooden benches along Beach Drive, plus one built on the overlook's 600-foot-long promenade, are placed for viewing the sunset behind the Olympics. Steps from the promenade lead to tide pools on the beach below. Across Beach Drive is the former hillside estate of Emma and Ferdinand Schmitz, now Me-Kwa-Mooks Park, where you can spread a picnic on the tables under the trees.

Ferdinand and Emma Schmitz were early pioneers, arriving in Seattle from Germany in 1887. In 1907, they purchased the hillside that now comprises the

Me-Kwa-Mooks Park, and built a seven-bedroom mansion over-looking Puget Sound. The home, called Sans Souci (French for "without care"), was demolished and left to ruin and tangled vines after it suffered damage in the 1964 earthquake. In 1971, the city of Seattle purchased the overgrown site and began restoration of the grounds, once landscaped by Ferdinand Schmitz with extensive plantings, orchards, and a pool.

Me-Kwa-Mooks Park is a shaded, green square at the base of a steep, wooded hillside. You can catch the spectacular views of Puget Sound from the park's three picnic tables. If you feel adventurous, explore the overgrown paths that ascend the hill and wind among the foundations, sidewalks, and steps of the former mansion.

Me-Kwa-Mooks was a nearby ancestral Indian village and means "shaped like a bear's head" in the Nisqually dialect. It also describes the geographical shape of the area that includes Alki Point and the Duwamish Head.

JOSE RIZAL PARK

A narrow view bluff.

South Judkins and 12th Avenue
South, Seattle.
684-4081

Located on the northwest
corner of Beacon Hill, west of
the Pacific Medical Center.
From I-5, take the James Street
exit. Drive east on James up the
hill to Boren Avenue and turn
south (right). At 12th Avenue
South, turn south (right).
Continue across the Jose Rizal
Bridge and keep right. The park
is on the west side of the street.

Hours: Daily, dawn to dusk.
Tables, barbecues, water, and
    restrooms are available.
Bus routes: 1, 60

Jose Rizal Park, only a few minutes from downtown Seattle, is
an ideal spot to picnic and view
glorious sunsets. This vantage
point overlooks the Kingdome and
the industrial section south of
downtown and boasts an expansive view of the city, Elliott Bay,
and the Olympic Mountains—
dramatic props for an evening sky.
The park was created on land that
was once a tangle of blackberry
bushes and weeds. Today, park
facilities include a picnic shelter
with tables and grills, play equipment for children, walking trails,
and an open-air amphitheater. The
tables angled to face the mountains
and water are the best places for picnicking.

At the request of Seattle's large and active Filipino community, the
parks department in 1974 named this park in honor of a national
hero of the Philippines, Dr. Jose Rizal. Born in 1861, Rizal received
a medical degree, and wrote poetry and two popular novels criticiz-
ing Spanish tyranny in the Philippines. His work was considered
subversive by the ruling Spanish regime and in 1896, accused of
helping instigate the Filipino insurrection, he was executed. A bust

of Rizal can be found on the park's upper slope.

Along the eastern border of the park is a colorful abstract mosaic by Seattle University professor and artist, Val Laigo. Its three upright panels depict the tricolor Philippine flag, the United States flag, and an abstract constellation of stars symbolizing the diversity of Philippine culture. Laigo's Filipino heritage and years of study in Mexico serve as inspiration for many of his works.

KUBOTA GARDEN

A large Japanese garden with Northwest native plants.

Corner of Renton Avenue South and 51st Avenue South, Seattle.
684-4081

Located south of Rainier Beach. From I-5, take the Swift Avenue/Albro Place exit. Head south and east on Swift Avenue South (it becomes South Myrtle Street) to Martin Luther King, Jr. Way South. Turn south (right) and drive one block to Renton Avenue South. Turn east (left) and drive one block past 51st Avenue South to Lindsay Place. Turn south (right) to the park.

Hours: Daily, dawn to dusk.
No tables, barbecues, water, or restrooms.
Bus routes: 42, 49, 106

Kubota Garden, a serene, 20-acre Japanese landscape that features Northwest native plants, is one of the Seattle Park Department's newer acquisitions. The garden was a gift to the city from the estate of the late Fujitaro Kubota, who spent years creating and tending this and other Northwest Japanese gardens (see Seattle University, page 211).

The garden, situated on two hills, is approached by following a path that encircles the property. Only a portion of the grounds has been designed in the style of a Japanese garden. This developed section lies beyond a vacant house. The remainder of the property, the southern half covered with trees, is to be landscaped in the future. Many hours of volunteer effort by the Friends of Kubota Garden are largely responsible for the garden's ongoing restoration and maintenance.

Because the developed portion lies hidden behind the house, you won't receive an overall sense of the park when you first arrive. But

247

if you descend into the garden from the path to the north of the house near the park entrance, you will be rewarded with a scene out of old Japan.

Water spills over a man-made waterfall to fill the pond that lies under a graceful crimson bridge. In the spring, blooming cherry trees add a delicate touch, and in the summer, yellow irises bloom at the pond's edge. Large flat rocks there provide a place to sit and enjoy your picnic.

If you climb the path to the top of the hill behind the pond, you will pass an occasional boulder engraved with Japanese characters. A stone bench along the way provides an opportunity to stop and reflect on the garden view below.

At the crest of this hill, two additional benches are protected by a wooden umbrella. You could open your Japanese *bento* (portable lunch) here or return to spread your blanket in one of several grassy spots beneath the alder trees below.

On any given day in Japan, parks, beaches, mountain trails, and temple grounds are filled with couples and families sharing their bentos and admiring the view. Kubota Garden captures this spirit perfectly.

LINCOLN PARK

*A large wooded bluff and long beachfront in West Seattle
full of recreational possibilities.*

Fauntleroy SW and SW
Webster, Seattle.
684-4081

Located on the shore of Puget
Sound in West Seattle. From
I-5, take the West Seattle exit
and follow the signs to
Fauntleroy Avenue SW and the
Fauntleroy ferry dock. The park
entrance and parking lots are
just north of the entrance to the
ferry dock.

Hours: Daily, 6:00 A.M. to
  10:00 P.M. Colman Pool:
  Open mid-June to
  September. Call 684-7494
  for information.
Tables, barbecues, water, and
  restrooms are available.
Bus routes: 34, 54

You can hike, play ball, pitch
horseshoes, swim, ride a bicycle,
play tennis, and even picnic in
Lincoln Park. This wonderfully
diverse park also has tall forests
of cedar, redwood, and Douglas
fir; wide meadows and sweeps of
lawn; rocky beaches and dramatic,
wooded lookouts over Puget
Sound. The range of activities and
variety of picnic spots to be found
make this place ideal for either a
small, intimate picnic or for a large
gathering of family and friends.

On the upper, wooded level, you
will find ball fields, fitness stations,
playgrounds, horseshoe pits, a
wading pool, and several picnic
shelters. Occasional benches are
placed along the upper bluff for you to enjoy the water views.

Biking and walking paths connect many of the park's facilities. At
the north, a steep, switchback trail follows the bluff down to the
beach. At the south end of the park, an easier trail leads to the
water's edge and the beach.

A mile-long sea-level promenade joins the north and south trails. It follows a driftwood-strewn beach where, at low tide, you can dig for clams or search the tide pools for sea cucumbers and anemones. The beach is filled with uprooted stumps that protect you when you stop to watch the waves crash during a blustery winter afternoon.

On sunny days, two shelters and several tables at the south end of the beach walk are the best places to picnic. You'll have clear views of the Vashon ferry, Puget Sound, and the Olympic Mountains, as well as ready access to a sandy beach. During the winter months, you can picnic by a warming fire in the wood stoves of shelters 1 and 2 on the park's south bluff. From October to March, the shelters are available on a first-come, first-served basis.

Colman Pool, a heated saltwater pool located along the beachfront promenade, is open to the public during the summer months. The pool is open to the sky but is protected from the wind by a glass wall. Tables and benches for picnicking are placed just outside the pool.

MUSEUM OF FLIGHT

Outside the museum, a grassy knoll for picnicking in the shadow of a B-47.

9404 East Marginal Way South, Seattle.
764-5720

Located west of I-5 and Boeing Field and between downtown Seattle and Sea-Tac International Airport. From I-5, take the East Marginal Way South exit (Exit 158). Head west from the exit and drive two blocks to East Marginal Way. Turn north (right). The museum is about four blocks on the right.

Hours: Daily, 10:00 A.M. to 5:00 P.M. Thursday until 9:00 P.M.
Water and restrooms are available. No tables, barbecues.
Museum fees: Adults, $4.00; Youths, $3.00; Children $2.00; Children under 6 years of age are free.
Bus route: 174

The Museum of Flight, located ten miles south of downtown Seattle, explores our fascination with flight. You don't have to be an aviation expert to enjoy the museum's impressive collection housed inside the Boeing Company's original Red Barn and a new glass-and-steel complex. Outside, planes are taking off and landing at the adjacent Boeing Field. The museum is the only one of its kind located next to a working airfield.

Tour guides, many of them retired military and commercial airline pilots and attendants, bring the exhibits to life. Twenty-two aircraft, including a replica of the Wright brothers' original glider, an Aerocar III, and the first F-5 Supersonic fighter, are suspended from the ceiling in the six-story, glass-enclosed Great Gallery. Several more planes are on display at the floor level, including the Douglas A-4F Skyhawk, one of the jets used by the Blue Angels. Connected to the Great Gallery is the lovingly restored Red Barn, where the Boeing Company first opened shop in 1916. There, you will trace the history of flight from its early beginnings through 1938. Lifelike figures assemble old wood-and-fabric wings, a restored drafting room and office appear ready for plane orders, and a beautifully crafted 1917 Curtiss Jenny biplane rests nearby. A replica of an 1895 glider hangs from the barn's ceiling. Although the museum is located adjacent to the Boeing Company's flight research facilities, it is not formally connected to the aviation giant. The museum's collection does emphasize the Pacific Northwest's rich aviation history and significant contributions to flight. Give yourself at least two hours to tour the exhibits.

Over the next five years, the museum will continue to alter its exhibits, creating some of the most engaging interactive displays to be found in any flight museum. The recently opened Hangar—a flying school for children—is a popular educational field trip. Here, children can explore the principles of flight by manipulating controls in a real cockpit.

There are no food concessions in the museum, so be sure to pack your own food supplies. Spread your picnic outside in the company of historic planes on the small patch of grass behind the museum building. Besides having an Air Force B-47, an Army Air Corps B-17F Flying Fortress (star of the movie *Memphis Belle*), and an Alaska Airlines mail carrier as part of your atmosphere outdoors, you will be able to watch the frequent takeoffs and landings at Boeing Field. The site of Seattle's first powered airplane flight (and crash!) in 1910, Boeing Field today is one of the country's ten busiest airfields.

SOUTH SEATTLE COMMUNITY COLLEGE ARBORETUM

Expansive views of downtown skyline.
The future site of the Seattle Chinese Garden.

6000 16th Avenue SW, Seattle.
764-5398

Located on the campus of South Seattle Community College in West Seattle. From I-5, take the Spokane Street/West Seattle exit. Go over the West Seattle bridge to the Delridge Way exit. Drive under the bridge and head south on Delridge Way to SW Dawson Street, across from Delridge Playfield. Turn east and follow Dawson to 16th Avenue SW. The community college is on your left. Park at the far north end of the parking lot.

Hours: Daily, 8:00 A.M. to dusk.
Restrooms and water are
   located in the college
   buildings. No tables or
   barbecues.
Bus route: 50

Uncover one of West Seattle's little-known treasures — the arboretum on the northern edge of South Seattle Community College's campus in West Seattle. The demonstration gardens, wooden gazebo, and vast grassy meadow rest in a state of undisturbed beauty, apparently off most everyone's beaten path. Situated on top of a ridge, the site commands a sweeping view of distant downtown and Elliott Bay.

Planting in the 12-acre arboretum began in earnest in 1983. Five distinct gardens have been established and ambitious designs for five additional demonstration projects, including a classical Chinese garden and a children's hands-on garden, are in various stages of planning and installation.

Most of the plants in the arboretum are labeled should you wish to identify a species for your home garden.

Changing color will greet you as you walk through the seasonal flower beds of the formal Entry Gardens. In the Sensory Garden, plants are selected for their texture, taste, and fragrance. More than 100 varieties of roses bloom in the Helen Sutton Rose Garden. Practical information on design, plant choice, irrigation systems, and mulching techniques can be found in the Water Conservation Garden. Following your tour of these gardens, head for the Gazebo Garden for the arboretum's prime picnic site. Spread your picnic on the wooden benches of the large gazebo and take in the grand view of the entire arboretum and downtown skyscrapers. Your efforts to visit this uncrowded site will be rewarded.

In the undeveloped meadow north of the arboretum, the city of Seattle, along with sister city Chongqing in southcentral China, will soon begin work on the first outdoor classical Chinese garden in the United States. Plans to build the garden began in 1986, but were put on hold after the events in Tiananmen Square in 1989.

In China, classical gardens have evolved for more than 2,000 years and express a vast accumulation of art, poetry, history, philosophy, and architecture. In addition to selected plants and contoured landscapes, garden views incorporate meeting halls, bridges, grottoes, stone lanterns, waterfalls, and pavilions. Seattle's Chinese garden will have these elements and yet reflect the informal natural garden style of Chongqing.

The college considers the chance to help maintain the garden a unique opportunity for the more than 800 students enrolled in its environmental horticultural program — the largest in the Northwest.

BELLEFIELDS NATURE PARK

Three miles of trails through urban marshland and deciduous woods.

1905 118th Avenue SE,
Bellevue.
455-6881

Located one mile south of
downtown Bellevue. From
I-405, take the SE Eighth Street
exit (Exit 12). Drive west on
SE Eighth to 118th Avenue SE.
Turn left (south) and drive
about ½ mile to the park's
parking lot on your right.

Hours: Daily, 8:00 A.M. to dusk.
One fire pit is available. No
   tables, water, or restrooms.
Bus route: 220

In Bellefields Nature Park you
can feel lost in the wilderness,
though this urban park has a busy
street, two freeways, and the
bustling city of Bellevue just
beyond its borders. Traffic from
I-405 can be seen and heard from
a few points on the trails, but not
enough to be intrusive.

The 48-acre park along Mercer
Slough contains marshes, deciduous woodlands, and gurgling
water, plus a three-mile network
of trails with names like Night-
shade Avenue, Water Birch Loop,
and Skunk Cabbage Lane. Encroaching shrubs surround the trails,
but the tangle is kept cleared from the one-mile perimeter path.
Before 1917, much of this low-lying area was under water. With the
opening of the ship canal, Lake Washington was lowered nine feet,
exposing some of the land bordering the slough. The ground can be
wet even during a dry summer, so wear appropriate footgear.

Volunteer groups have helped the parks department make several
improvements to the grounds, adding wooden bridges, boardwalks,
benches, and totem poles. Near the entrance from 118th Avenue SE,
six benches arranged around a fire pit are used as an open-air

classroom for school groups on a nature outing. A delightful place to picnic is on the deserted bench in a grassy clearing along the bank of the slough. This peaceful spot is also a good perch for watching the variety of ducks and other waterfowl attracted to the wetlands.

The Mercer Slough, 1½ miles long, meanders past Bellefields Nature Park on its route from Kelsey Creek to Lake Washington. If you've never tried kayaking, the quiet-flowing slough is a great place to start. You can put in your kayak from the opposite bank at the Mercer Slough Boat Launch, 3000 Bellevue Way SE, and paddle up and across the slough to the park.

Blueberries thrive in the lowland's moist soil. Overlake Blueberry Farm lies across the slough, just north of the boat launch at 2127 Bellevue Way SE. The farm sells fresh blueberries by the pound from mid-July to mid-September and will readily share their recipes with you. A few blueberry shrubs also grow in the nature park.

Bellefields' trees are deciduous, so try to visit the park when it is most colorful in spring, summer, and fall.

CARILLON POINT

A privately developed waterfront community.

2350 Carillon Point, Kirkland.
889-2377

Located on Lake Washington south of Kirkland, one mile north of the Hwy 908/Hwy 520 interchange. Take the Hwy 908 east/Kirkland exit north from Hwy 520. Travel north about a mile to the third stoplight at the corner of Lake Washington Boulevard NE and Lakeview Drive and the entrance to Carillon Point.

Hours: Daily, 11:00 A.M. to
11:00 P.M.
Tables, water, and restrooms
are available. No barbecues.
Bus routes: 251, 254, 256

If you haven't visited the eastern shore of Lake Washington just south of Kirkland in a while, you owe yourself a trip. The area has changed dramatically, especially at Carillon Point, where the shoreline has been transformed into an inviting, self-contained community.

At the lakeside, a lamp-lined promenade stretches along a public marina with rowing and sailing clubs and rental boats. Benches on the promenade are inviting places from which to watch the boating activity. Historical plaques along the walk tell of early shipbuilding at John Anderson's Lake Washington Shipyards and of the social activities at the Atlanta Park dance pavilion that was once located here.

Up the steps from the marina and promenade, cafes, pizzerias, restaurants, elegant shops, a luxury hotel, and even a bank and post office surround a central plaza. You can spread your picnic on the tables in the plaza and watch the sunset as carillon bells chime the hour.

The first permanent settlement along the east side of Lake Washington began in 1872 when Henry French moved from crowded Seattle (population: 2,000) and staked his claim. He was soon followed by others, including Peter Kirk, Kirkland's namesake, and, in 1901, Captain John Anderson, founder of the Lake Washington Shipyards. For over 50 years, near the site of Carillon Point, the shipyard built lake- and ocean-going ferries and World War II seaplane tenders. During the Alaska-Yukon-Pacific Exposition in 1909, Captain Anderson ran a ferry service from the east side of the lake to the University of Washington campus, where more than 3.7 million people attended the exposition.

Kirkland's waterfront trolley leaves from the Watermark Hotel at Carillon Point and provides a 12-minute ride north to the Peter Kirk Art Gallery and additional parks and boutiques in downtown Kirkland. The city retains many historic landmarks and artifacts, including Captain Anderson's ferry clock, which continues to keep perfect time at its original location on the corner of Kirkland Avenue and Lake Street. Kirkland's historic homes and the first national co-op cannery (640 Eighth Avenue) built by the Works Progress Administration in 1936 lend themselves to an informative, self-guided car tour. The Kirkland Cannery (828-4521), now privately owned, smokes and cans freshly caught salmon, tuna, sturgeon, and oysters year-round; and from early January to mid-September, the catch of local sportfishers as well. Although the cannery does not conduct tours, you can watch the activity through the glass doors of the retail room. Picnic fare, including smoked salmon pâté and Nova lox, can be purchased at the cannery. The Historical Commission of Kirkland (822-5029) or the Greater Kirkland Chamber of Commerce (822-7066) can provide information for your tour.

A growing number of public sculptures in Kirkland provide a worthwhile diversion after your waterside picnic. Local galleries and restaurants have maps of the town that include the locations of six public artworks, many on long-term loan from local businessman and philanthropist William G. Ballantine.

If you arrive by car, you can park free for three hours in Carillon Point's parking lot.

CHATEAU STE. MICHELLE WINERY

A bit of Napa Valley north of Seattle.

14111 NE 145th Street,
Woodinville.
488-1133

Located south of Woodinville. From I-405, take Exit 23A (SR 522, Monroe-Wenatchee) to the Woodinville exit. Turn south (right) off the exit and continue three blocks to NE 175th Street. Turn west (right) and follow the road to the stop sign. Turn south (left) on Hwy 202 and drive approximately two miles to the winery entrance.

Hours: Daily, 10:00 A.M. to
    4:30 P.M. The grounds and
    shop are open late during
    scheduled evening concerts
    and performances.
Tables, restrooms, and water
    are available. No barbecues.
Handicapped access.
Entrance fees for the
    amphitheater for some
    performances.
Bus routes: 307, 311, 372, 931

A little wine, a little music, a French chateau—only 30 minutes north of Seattle by car. Spread a blanket on the soft grass under tall shade trees at Chateau Ste. Michelle winery for a romantic, lazy afternoon. During the summer, music and theater performances take place in the grassy, open-air amphitheater. With its gracious surroundings, the winery is a relaxing place to meet friends for a picnic supper and concert on a warm, summer evening.

Chateau Ste. Michelle's grounds were once part of the Hollywood Farm estate of lumber baron Fred Stimson, and some of the original 1912 buildings still remain. The Olmsted Brothers, a well-known landscaping firm that shaped much of Seattle's park system in the early part of the century, created the formal gardens for the Stimson estate. The restored grounds with trout ponds and fountains, mature trees and unusual plantings, form outdoor rooms for strolling and exploring. Children love to roam these garden nooks and crannies.

Though virtually all Chateau Ste. Michelle's grapes are grown on the sunny Columbia Plateau, a small vineyard at the entrance to the winery transports you to wine country. The French country chateau was built in 1976 when the winery established its Woodinville facility, and houses its tasting and barrel rooms. The winery's well-stocked gift shop encourages picnics, offering imaginative picnic fare such as truffles, pâté, and pasta salad, as well as delicious basics—brownies, bread, cheese, fruit, and, of course, wine. Free tastings and cellar tours are conducted frequently during the day between 10:00 A.M. and 4:30 P.M. Cooking demonstrations and other special events are held throughout the year.

The winery is a popular destination for cyclists. From Seattle, the Burke-Gilman Trail follows the western shore of Lake Washington north to Logboom Park in Kenmore. Cyclists must take a short ride on an arterial before joining the Sammamish River Trail, which leads right to Ste. Michelle. The winery is just off the trail at NE 145th.

Washington's wine industry, though young, is producing some outstanding wines. For an introduction to the variety and character of Washington wines, tour some of the other wineries that have established facilities in the Woodinville area. These include Columbia (488-2776), French Creek (486-1900), Salmon Bay (483-9436), and Tagaris (486-9463) wineries.

CHISM BEACH PARK

A small, wooded park with beachside tables.

1175 96th Avenue SE, Bellevue.
455-6881

Located on the eastern shore of Lake Washington about one mile southwest of downtown Bellevue. From I-405, take the NE Eighth Street exit west to Bellevue Way. Turn south on Bellevue Way. Turn west on Main Street and drive one short block past the first stoplight. Turn south on 101st Avenue SE. Follow the curving road to the Chism Beach Park sign.

Hours: Dawn to dusk, daily.
Tables, barbecues, water, and
    restrooms are available.
Handicapped access.
Bus route: None

Chism Beach Park is a small, waterfront park in a quiet Bellevue neighborhood. A terraced lawn sweeps down to the water's edge to a roped swimming area and diving platform, picnic tables, barbecues, and a children's play area—ingredients for an entire day's summer fun.

From the parking lot at the top of the lawn, two steep paths descend to a small beach with several picnic tables and barbecues. From the beach, a narrow strip of grass between the wooded hillside and the shore of Lake Washington leads to several tables under the trees for picnicking at the water's edge. These are the best tables, with the lake lapping nearby, and expansive views of Mercer Island and, farther north, of Seattle's downtown skyscrapers just visible on the horizon.

At the peak of summer, you might not have the pick of the tables. You can spread a blanket on the grassy terraced hillside shaded by madronas and watch the beachside activity from above.

GENE F. COULON MEMORIAL PARK

A multi-use park with a variety of waterfront diversions.

1201 Lake Washington
Boulevard North, Renton.
235-2560

Located on the extreme
southeast tip of Lake
Washington north of Renton.
From I-405, take the NE Park
Avenue and Sunset Boulevard
NE exit and head west toward
the lake. Follow the signs to
Coulon Memorial Park and
turn north (right) on Lake
Washington Boulevard North.

Hours: Daily, 7:00 A.M. to
 sunset.
Tables, barbecues, water, and
 restrooms are available.
Bus routes: 106, 107, 109, 147

Coulon Park has something for
everyone and room in which to do
it. The mile-long waterfront park
embraces fishing piers, a duck
preserve, covered picnic areas, an
Ivar's restaurant and food concession, boat launch and rentals, and
sandy beaches with supervised
swimming. All summer, kayaks,
canoes, sailboards, jet skis, and
sailboats maneuver offshore.

This pristine park, with sweeping
views of the southernmost shores
of Lake Washington, the Bellevue
hills, and distant Seattle, is
organized into two sections: a
long, north park and a shorter,
south park.

The park's northern arm extends by means of a ¾-mile walking and
biking path that follows the crest of a grass-covered slope along the
shore. The path provides access to the Ivar's food concession, several covered picnic pavilions, a swimming area, canoe launch with
boat-rental facility, and fishing pier. The best place to picnic in the
park is the large group pavilion located north of Ivar's. Here you can
choose tables on the sunny deck that overlooks the water or, in

winter, picnic on the sheltered tables and benches that surround a sunken fire pit and build a roaring fire.

A small wooden bridge across John's Creek separates the north and south sections of the park. Much of the activity in the south end centers around the tennis and volleyball courts, horseshoe pits, and motorboat launch. The large, sandy beach has a bathhouse and supervised swimming with a second food concession, picnic shelter, and playground nearby. The tiny duck island just off the beach is closed to humans when the ducks are nesting.

GROVELAND BEACH PARK

A terraced, shaded waterfront.

SE 57th Street and 80th Avenue SE, Mercer Island.
236-3545

Located on the west side of Mercer Island. From I-90, take the Island Crest Way exit and drive south. At SE 44th Street, turn west and drive one block to West Mercer Way. Turn south on West Mercer Way to SE 57th Place. The park is straight ahead.

Hours: Daily, dawn to dusk.
Tables, barbecues, water, and restrooms are available.
Bus route: 201

This charming, underused park lies on the west shore of Mercer Island. With views west across Lake Washington of the great undeveloped toe of Seward Park, you can almost envision this land in its wild state. In the distance, jets flying toward Sea-Tac Airport look like giant soaring birds.

From the parking lot, a short steep path winds down the wooded hillside. Near the top of the path, a children's play area with teeter-totters, rocking horses, swings, and a climbing dome occupies a leveled clearing. Just off the parking lot, a lone table nestled among the trees is a secluded place to picnic.

At the lakeshore, two picnic tables are set in a peaceful little glade shaded by tall fir trees. The long pier bordering a swimming area is a good place to sit and watch both swimmers and boats.

JUANITA BAY PARK

A vast, sunny bank overlooking wetlands.

Market Street and NE 106th Street, Juanita.
296-2966

Located on the east side of Lake Washington, north of Kirkland. From I-405, take the NE 116th Street exit. Head west on 116th toward Lake Washington to 98th Avenue NE. Turn south (left) onto 98th, which turns into Market Street. Drive approximately ½ mile to the park.

Hours: Daily, dawn to dusk.
No tables, barbecues, or water.
One portable toilet is available.
Bus route: 255

For serenity and isolation, picnic on the soft grass beneath graceful old willows at Juanita Bay Park. To the west, beyond tall marsh grasses and trees, Lake Washington gleams in the distance.

This 65-acre park was once a golf course, but now its expansive green lawn and wetlands are a favorite bird-watching area. In the spring and fall, more than 20 species of migrating waterfowl use the banks of Lake Washington as a way station. Other wildlife make their home in the park. A bridge that was once part of the main road from Juanita to Kirkland (but is now closed to vehicles) allows you to walk over the marsh for a closer look. Below the bridge you may see beaver dams and the tracks of raccoons, deer, opossum, or muskrat. During the summer, the Kirkland Parks and Recreation Department (859-3350) offers guided nature walks in the park to children and their parents.

From the park, it looks like there is a way to get closer to Lake Washington, but appearances are deceiving. There is no beach and a search for a path will only mire your shoes in ooze.

KELSEY CREEK PARK

*This park provides a pleasant introduction
to nature, agriculture, and frontier history.*

13204 SE Eighth Place,
Bellevue.
455-7688

Located southeast of downtown
Bellevue. From I-405, take the
SE Eighth Street exit and head
east under the freeway.
Continue straight east at the
Lake Hill Connector
intersection. The road becomes
SE Seventh Place. Turn north
on 128th Avenue SE and drive
to SE Fourth Place; turn east
(right). The park and parking
lot are two blocks ahead.

Hours: Daily, dawn to dusk.
Tables, barbecues, water, and
     restrooms are available.
Bus routes: 220, 253 (from
     downtown Seattle) to
     Bellevue Transit Center.
     Transfer to the 920 transit
     van.

This family-oriented park will
fascinate people of all ages. It
offers hiking trails through
wooded hills, a jogging track, two
petting barns, a formal Japanese
garden, a restored log cabin, and
a bubbling creek.

The 80-acre park is named after
Henry E. Kelsey, a New York
schoolteacher who, in 1884,
became the first teacher of Bellevue and Mercer Island children.
By 1888, he had saved enough
money to buy 160 acres of land
nearby, complete with the creek
that still bears his name. Later, a
more promising teaching position
lured him to Hawaii.

Start by crossing the bridge
directly south of the parking lot
and continue up and over a hill, to a pleasant one-mile loop trail. It
leads through the woods and over a twisting creek where salmon
continue to return to spawn. Two lone tables along the trail, about ¼
mile and ½ mile from the bridge, provide secluded places to picnic.

Joggers have their own ½-mile oval track behind the hill and the barns.

West of the parking lot, the Yao Park Sister City Oriental Garden draws Japanese gardening fans. Benches in a weathered pavilion and others placed among the trees and giant pussywillows near the garden's pond make tranquil places for spreading your lunch. Stone lanterns and gently curving paths enhance the garden's quiet mood.

West of the Oriental garden, a wide meadow with several tables and barbecues could accomodate a large family gathering. Or you may wish to spread your blanket under the trees on the hill. From here you have a prime view north of most of the park.

West across the meadow stands the 1888 Fraser log cabin, which was relocated from its original homestead site and reassembled in the park. You can walk around it and peer into the windows at the period furnishings.

Before its development into a park, Kelsey Creek had been a working farm for over 50 years and appropriately it now contains two large, white barns located west of the park entrance. Spring is the time for children to visit the farmyard and see the newborn calves, kids, chicks, bunnies, and piglets.

The Bellevue Parks Department office is located west of the barns. Check here for information about pony classes and guided tours of the park and farm.

LUTHER BURBANK COUNTY PARK

*A large, sunny park with a grassy slope to water's edge
and an enchanting play area.*

2040 84th Avenue SE,
Mercer Island.
296-4232

Located on the northeast shore
of Mercer Island, north of I-90.
From I-90 on Mercer Island,
take the Island Crest Way exit,
drive north to SE 26th Street
and turn north one block onto
84th Avenue SE. Parking lots
are located at the north and
south park entrances.

Hours: Daily, 8:30 A.M. to dusk.
Tables, barbecues, water, and
    restrooms are available.
Bus routes: 226 or 235 to
    Mercer Island Park-and-
    Ride stop at North Mercer
    Way and 80th Avenue SE.
    Park is a five-block walk

The Duwamish Indians were perhaps the first to picnic and forage on Mercer Island. They never encamped overnight, however, because they believed that when night fell, the island disappeared below the surface of Lake Washington. You probably won't be staying overnight either, but you can still have a great day foraging, picnicking, and playing.

Do reserve an entire day to discover for yourself the many delights of this Mercer Island park. You will find the north and south sections of the park have distinctly different functions separated by an amphitheater at the center of the park. The southern half is devoted to activity—tennis, sunning, swimming, boating, fishing, kite-flying, barbecuing, children's play, and (with a permit from the park offices on the grounds) metal-detecting. The waterfront area has a grassy bank that leads to a supervised sandy beach and roped swimming area. North of the swimming area, a tree-lined trail takes you to several boat docks for day use.

You can picnic at several tables by the beach or on those among the trees above the tennis courts. Game tables, including three with built-in chess boards, are protected under a glass shelter.

The northern half of the park has been left in a more natural state characterized by tall grass, thick mounds of blackberry vines, and wetlands. Several trees, dating from the time when the park was a boarding school for boys that raised all its own food, bear fruit for the taking. A brick house, once the dormitory for the boarding school, now houses the park offices. Along the shore north of the park offices, several secluded clearings make ideal places for a picnic for two. Look for the No. 6 sign for a sandy lakeside spot.

The children's play area at Luther Burbank is particularly creative. Tunnels, towers, swings, bridges, ramps, and firemen poles span a sandy pit. Regrettably, the popular sliding pulley was removed during the playground's expansion.

NEWCASTLE BEACH PARK

One of Bellevue's newest waterfront parks.

4400 Lake Washington
Boulevard SE, Bellevue.
455-6881

Located two exits south of the
I-90/I-405 interchange in
Bellevue. From I-405, take the
112th Avenue SE exit (No. 9).
Follow the signs located at the
exit intersection to the park.

Hours: Daily, dawn to dusk.
Tables, water, and restrooms
  are available. No barbecues.
Bus route: 340. The park is nine
  blocks north of the Newport
  Hills Park-and-Ride stop.

Newcastle Beach is one of the few stretches of Lake Washington shoreline that hasn't been snapped up by developers. Its woods provide shelter for muskrat, river otter, deer, and several species of birds, including bald eagles that are often spotted on the tops of the tall fir trees east of the picnic area. The woods border the north and south sides of the park and channel the view toward Lake Washington and across the water to Mercer Island. A long expanse of lawn reaching from the parking lot to a sandy beach cuts a wide, open slice through the center of the park.

The park is named for one of three coal-mining towns that sprang up in 1868 after coal was discovered nearby. More than 150 million tons of coal and waste rock were mined from 1868 to 1963 and, in the days before rail, transported to steam barges on Lake Washington just south of the park. At one time, the town of Newcastle boasted the second-largest population in Washington, after Seattle.

Walking paths crisscross the park. A short loop trail leaves the park from the car turnaround at the end of the drive. It crosses a small stream and curves through hawthorn and ferns. One path off the loop trail leads to a secluded beach just big enough for a picnic for two.

Picnic tables for a large gathering are available on the sunny lawn. North of the lawn, a children's play area has a colorful train, a teeter-totter, sliding board, and swings. At the lake, wooden benches along the paved shore walk overlook the water, a fishing pier, and a sandy beach with a supervised swimming area. A bathhouse just up the steps from the beach has outdoor showers.

No fire pits or grills are available in the park, but there are two barrels for disposing of hot coals for those who bring their own grills. Pets are not permitted in the park between June 1 and September 15.

RADAR PARK

A grassy pinnacle on Cougar Mountain with expansive views.

SE Cougar Mountain Drive, Bellevue.
296-4232

Located southeast of Bellevue at the top of Cougar Mountain. From I-90, take Exit 11-A. Head south on 150th Avenue SE to SE Newport Way. Turn east (left) and follow Newport Way to 164th Avenue SE. Turn south (right) and follow the road up the mountain to Cougar Mountain Way. Turn east (left) and follow the road as it curves to SE 60th Street, turn south (right) and drive one block, then right again at SE Cougar Mountain Drive. Drive approximately ¾ mile to the Radar Park's entrance gate. Park in the lot across from the lone house.

Hours: Daily, 8:00 A.M. to dusk.
Tables, water, and restrooms
 are available. No barbecues.
Bus route: None.

Not only does Radar Park provide the "million-dollar view" of Mount Baker, the Cascade Mountains, and Lake Sammamish, but the site also occupies an interesting chapter in local history. During World War II, antiaircraft guns were mounted here to protect Issaquah and areas east from Japanese invasion. Later, Nike missiles and radar were installed. The guns, radar, and missiles are gone, but the breathtaking view remains.

The general public seldom drives the twisting roads to this remote spot, which is one of the area's best sites for a romantic, secluded picnic. Try to pick a day when mist and fog do not cling to the hills because, at 1,400 feet, this park often lies shrouded while lower elevations bask in sunlight.

Radar Park can be enjoyed in any season. In spring, it is scented with blossoms; in summer, the large, green lawn is bathed in sun.

Late summer and early fall are good times to gather red huckleberries and black raspberries. And because the park is situated so high, snow etched with animal tracks often covers the ground in winter.

Choose one of the widely spaced tables for your picnic. On days when the park is sunny, head for the two tables under the cool protection of a pair of weeping willows. A single table occupies the choice viewspot of Mount Baker, the Cascades, and Lake Sammamish. Another table is hidden in a grove on a small hill. A fifth table sits among the trees and foundation of the old radar installation. There are no grills, but you may bring your own hibachi.

Pickers will want to look for the patch of wild black raspberries and thimbleberries midway along the asphalt drive. Red huckleberry bushes grow by the picnic table with the view.

Across Cougar Mountain Drive from the gates to Radar Park, more than 25 miles of hiking and horseback riding trails wind through heavily wooded Cougar Mountain Regional Park. Cougar Mountain, one of the three Issaquah Alps, is marked with old prospector trails, stagecoach roads, railroads, and mine shafts. It also boasts its own ghost town, Old Newcastle, a once-thriving community of European immigrants. The town was founded in 1868 near the present-day corner of SE 71st Street and 138th Avenue SE.

Maps and information on Cougar Mountain trails are available from the King County Parks Department, the Issaquah Alps Trails Club, and the Mountaineers.

The caretaker closes the gates of Radar Park at dusk.

ST. EDWARD STATE PARK

Former seminary grounds on Lake Washington.

NE 145th Street and Juanita Drive NE, Kenmore.
823-2992

Located on the northeast shore of Lake Washington between Bothell and Kirkland. From I-405, take the NE 116th Street exit and drive west. Turn north on Juanita Drive and drive approximately 2½ miles. The park entrance will be on the left (west) side of the street. There is no sign announcing the park.

Hours: April 1 to October 15, 6:30 A.M. to 10:00 P.M.; October 16 to March 31, 8:00 A.M. to 5:00 P.M.
Tables, barbecues, water, and restrooms are available.
Bus routes: 26, 309, 920

The grounds of St. Edward State Park are large and varied: an outdoor wedding with 300 guests could be held in one corner of the lawn here and hardly be noticed by a couple enjoying a romantic picnic in the orchard. Although the park was dedicated back in 1978, its picnic tables and trails tend to be underused—people come here largely to use the pool or gym. Picnickers can enjoy the grounds without disturbance.

In the 1920s, Bishop Edward J. O'Dea, with funds from his own inheritance, purchased the property on which the park now stands. From 1931 until the last seminary class ended in 1976, the minor (college level) seminary educated young men studying for the Catholic priesthood before they entered the major (graduate-school level) seminary. After the seminary closed, eager developers hoped to acquire the property. In 1977, Archbishop Raymond G. Hunthausen negotiated with the state instead, thus preserving over 3,000 feet of green bank on Lake Washington, as well as the largest undeveloped plot of land left on the lake.

Today the former seminary grounds are used by men *and* women —
to drive golf balls, play tennis or handball, to swim, to walk along the
wooded trails. Marriages take place at the grotto. The park is also an
excellent place for identifying birds, plants, and small animals. Barn
owls often nest in the church steeple.

St. Edward contains 28 miles of trails, both marked and unmarked.
Following one near the picnic table by the south perimeter of the
lawn brings you to a lovely abandoned apple orchard. Tracing
another trail past the grotto from the west edge of the grounds takes
you through a wooded gully to the banks of the lake.

More than 30 picnic tables are scattered throughout the park. The
most desirable table is situated under the huge trees south of the
tennis courts.

Alcohol consumption is permitted in the park, though kegs of beer
are not allowed.

PICNIC SITES BY LOCATION

DOWNTOWN SEATTLE
Convention Place Station
Grand Central Arcade
Myrtle Edwards Park
Union Square Plaza
Washington State Ferry
   System
Waterfall Garden
Waterfront Streetcar

CENTRAL SEATTLE
(NORTH OF DOWNTOWN AND
SOUTH OF THE SHIP CANAL)
Center for Wooden Boats
Discovery Park
Foster Island
Madrona Park
Parsons Gardens
Seattle University
Smith Cove Park
Washington Park Arboretum

NORTH SEATTLE
(NORTH OF THE SHIP
CANAL)
Carl S. English, Jr., Botanical
   Garden
Center for Urban
   Horticulture

Gas Works Park
Meridian Park
NOAA Grounds
Sunset Hill Park
University of Washington
Woodland Park Zoological
   Gardens and Rose Garden

SOUTH SEATTLE
Jose Rizal Park
Kubota Garden
Museum of Flight

WEST SEATTLE
Emma Schmitz Memorial
   Overlook and Me-Kwa-
   Mooks Park
Lincoln Park
South Seattle Community
   College Arboretum

EASTSIDE
(EAST OF LAKE
WASHINGTON, NORTH TO
WOODINVILLE AND SOUTH
TO RENTON)
Bellefields Nature Park
Carillon Point
Chateau Ste. Michelle Winery

Chism Beach Park
Gene F. Coulon Memorial
    Park
Groveland Beach Park
Juanita Bay Park
Kelsey Creek Park
Luther Burbank County Park
Newcastle Beach Park
Radar Park
St. Edward State Park

Picnic Sites by Activity

VIEW SITES
Discovery Park
Emma Schmitz Overlook
Gas Works Park
Jose Rizal Park
Lincoln Park
Myrtle Edwards Park
NOAA Grounds
Radar Park
Smith Cove Park
South Seattle Community
    College Arboretum
Sunset Hill Park
Washington State Ferry
    System

SUNSET VIEWING
SITES
Carillon Point
Chism Beach Park
Discovery Park
Emma Schmitz Overlook
Gas Works Park
Gene F. Coulon Memorial
    Park
Groveland Beach Park
Jose Rizal Park
Sunset Hill Park

Washington State Ferry
    System

MOONRISE SITES
Gas Works Park
Madrona Park
Washington State Ferry
    System

ROMANTIC SITES
Chateau Ste. Michelle Winery
Discovery Park
Kubota Garden
Parsons Gardens
Radar Park
Seattle University
University of Washington
Washington Park Arboretum
Washington State Ferry
    System
Waterfall Garden
Woodland Park Zoological
    Gardens (Rose Garden)

NATURE PARKS
Bellefields Nature Park
Center for Urban Horti-
    culture (Montlake Fill)

Discovery Park
Foster Island
Juanita Bay Park
Lincoln Park
Radar Park
St. Edward State Park

SITES FOR FAMILIES
Center for Wooden Boats
Discovery Park
Gas Works Park
Gene F. Coulon Memorial
Park
Kelsey Creek Park
Luther Burbank County Park
Meridian Park
Museum of Flight
Newcastle Beach Park
South Seattle Community
College Arboretum
Waterfront Streetcar
Washington State Ferry
System
Woodland Park Zoological
Gardens (Rose Garden)

SITES FOR
LARGE GROUPS
Discovery Park
Gas Works Park

Gene F. Coulon Memorial
Park
Kelsey Creek Park
Lincoln Park
Luther Burbank County Park
Meridian Park
Newcastle Beach Park
St. Edward State Park

SITES FOR SUMMER
SUN AND SWIMMING
Chism Beach Park
Gene F. Coulon Memorial
Park
Groveland Beach Park
Lincoln Park (Colman Pool)
Luther Burbank County Park
Madrona Park
Newcastle Beach Park

BEST FOR
SPRING BLOSSOMS
Carl S. English, Jr., Botanical
Garden
Kubota Garden
Seattle University
University of Washington
Washington Park Arboretum

BEST FOR
FALL COLOR
Discovery Park
Kubota Garden
University of Washington
Washington Park Arboretum

SNUG WINTER SITES
Gas Works Park
Gene F. Coulon Memorial
   Park
Grand Central Arcade
Lincoln Park
Washington State Ferry
   System
Waterfall Garden
Waterfront Streetcar

FORMAL GARDEN
SITES
Carl S. English, Jr., Botanical
   Garden
Center for Urban
   Horticulture
Chateau Ste. Michelle Winery
Kelsey Creek Park
Meridian Park
Parsons Gardens
Seattle University
South Seattle Community
   College Arboretum

University of Washington
Washington Park Arboretum
Woodland Park Zoological
   Gardens (Rose Garden)

SITES WITH
PUBLIC ART
Convention Place Station
Gas Works Park
Jose Rizal Park
Myrtle Edwards Park
NOAA Grounds
Seattle University
University of Washington
Woodland Park Zoological
   Gardens

SITES WITH MUSIC
Chateau Ste. Michelle Winery
Union Square Plaza

SITES WITH
JAPANESE GARDENS
Kelsey Creek Park
Kubota Garden
Seattle University
Washington Park Arboretum

SITES NEAR MUSEUMS

Center for Wooden Boats
Discovery Park
Foster Island
Grand Central Arcade
Museum of Flight
University of Washington
Washington State Ferry
  System
Waterfall Garden
Waterfront Streetcar

SITES FOR BOAT WATCHING

Carillon Point
Carl S. English, Jr., Botanical
  Garden
Center for Wooden Boats
Foster Island
Gas Works Park
Gene F. Coulon Memorial
  Park
Groveland Beach Park
Lincoln Park
Luther Burbank County Park
Madrona Park
Myrtle Edwards Park
Washington State Ferry
  System

SITES WITH WALKING TRAILS

Bellefields Nature Park
Center for Urban
  Horticulture
Discovery Park
Foster Island
Kelsey Creek Park
Lincoln Park
NOAA Grounds
Radar Park
St. Edward State Park

SITES NEAR BIKING TRAILS

Chateau Ste. Michelle Winery
Discovery Park
Gas Works Park
Madrona Park
Myrtle Edwards Park
Newcastle Beach Park
Smith Cove Park
University of Washington
Washington Park Arboretum

SITES FOR BIRD-WATCHERS

Bellefields Nature Park
Center for Urban
  Horticulture

Discovery Park
Foster Island
Juanita Bay Park
Lincoln Park
NOAA Grounds
St. Edward State Park
Seattle University

SITES WITH BOAT DOCKING FACILITIES
Carillon Point
Gene F. Coulon Memorial
   Park
Luther Burbank County Park

SITES WHERE ALCOHOL IS ALLOWED
Chateau Ste. Michelle Winery
   (wine only)
St. Edward State Park
Union Square Plaza (from
   restaurants)

Sources for Picnic Foods

DOWNTOWN AND CENTRAL SEATTLE

Bavarian Meat Delicatessen
1920 Pike Place
Seattle
441-0942
*Sauerkraut, pickles, German deli
meats, sausages, bratwurst.*

Cucina Fresca
1904 Pike Place
Seattle
448-4758
*Rice balls, pasta salads, fresh
pasta, and sauces to go.*

DeLaurenti's Italian &
International Food Market
1435 First Avenue
Seattle
622-0141
*Cheeses, meats, salads, breads.
Unusual imported ingredients
such as orange and rose water.*

Dilettante Chocolates—
Broadway Restaurant
416 Broadway East
Seattle
329-6463
*Three special sandwiches made
daily on the premises: country-
smoked ham, turkey breast, and
market vegetable. Romanian
borscht and two other soup specials
are prepared daily.*

Elliott Bay Cafe
First Avenue South & South
Main Street
Seattle
682-6664
*Salads, desserts, deli and specialty
items.*

Exquisite Desserts
2800 East Madison Street
Seattle
328-0518
*Bakery items sweetened with fruit
juice concentrates.*

Ezell's Fried Chicken
501 23rd Avenue
Seattle
324-4141
*Great fried chicken, sweet potato
pie, baked beans, and pound cake.*

Frederick & Nelson Arcade
506 Pine Street
Seattle
382-8233
*Large deli and imported foods
selection.*

Fromagerie
4122 East Madison
Seattle
323-6110
*Specialty gourmet items, including
200 varieties of European and
American cheeses, espresso.*

Grand Central Baking
Company
214 First Avenue South
Seattle
622-3644
*Bakery items, sandwiches, salads,
soups, drinks to go.*

Gravity Bar (two locations as
follows:)
86 Pine Street
Seattle
443-9694

415 Broadway East
Seattle
325-7186
*Anything on the menu can be
prepared to go, including open-face
sandwiches with goat cheese, pine
nuts, and vegetables; plus salads
and wheat grass juice. Great
yogurt and fruit shakes.*

Julia's 14 Carrot Cafe
2305 Eastlake Avenue East
Seattle
324-1442
*Wholesome, freshly prepared foods
from their lunch menu. Try their
special 3-D sandwich.*

King Cafe
723 South King Street
Seattle
622-6373
*Dim sum, humbow, and barbecued
pork to go.*

Macheesmo Mouse
211 Broadway Avenue East
Seattle
325-0072
*Made-to-order chicken and
vegetarian burritos, enchiladas,
soft tacos, and salads to go.*

New York Deli
2801 East Madison
Seattle
328-0750
*Daily specials, soups, salads,
sandwiches.*

Peerless Pie (three central
locations as follows:)
1930 Pike Place
Seattle
443-1801

Columbia Center
701 Fifth Avenue
Seattle
386-5855

434 Broadway East
Seattle
323-0476
*Chicken pot pie, Tuscan taco pot
pie, different berry pies every week.*

The Pike Place Creamery
1514 Pike Place
Seattle
622-5029
*Cheeses, yogurt, raw Guernsey
milk.*

The Souk
1916 Pike Place
Seattle
441-1666
*Middle Eastern and African spices
and ingredients.*

Surrogate Hostess
746 19th East
Seattle
324-1944
*Sandwiches, soups, salads, breads,
desserts, specialty items.*

Three Girls Bakery
1514 Pike Place
Seattle
622-1045
*Sandwiches on homemade bread,
soups, potato salad, cookies, fresh
bread, and pies to go.*

Toshi's Teriyaki
1631 East Olive Way
Seattle
726-0141
*Take-out chicken and beef
teriyaki, coleslaw, and rice.*

Uwajimaya
Sixth Avenue South and
South King Street
Seattle
624-6248
*Fresh shellfish, Japanese foods to
go, endamame, Calpico.*

Viet-Wah Supermarket
1032 South Jackson Street
Seattle
329-1399
*Large market with Thai,
Taiwanese, Korean, and Filipino
fresh and packaged foods and
ingredients. Chinese herbalist on
premises.*

Wa Sang Company
663 South King Street
Seattle
622-2032
*Small shop in International
District selling Chinese,
Indonesian, Korean, Filipino, and
Thai ingredients.*

Westlake Center Foodcourt
1601 Fifth Avenue
Seattle
467-1600
*Numerous independent food
counters with a variety of ethnic
and American take-out items,
located on the top floor of
Westlake Center.*

NORTH SEATTLE
A La Francaise
2609 University Village
Seattle
524-9300
Breads, croissants, soups, pizza. Available by special order in late fall are limited-edition tarts made from a particular variety of apple once loved by Napoleon and Louis XIV, and now grown by a physician on Bainbridge Island.

Brie and Bordeaux
2108 North 55th
Seattle
633-3538
Cheeses, deli and specialty items, espresso, wine, and beer.

Buddy's Homesick Cafe
8420 Greenwood Avenue
North
Seattle
784-6430
Pick up anything on the menu for your picnic, including chicken fried steak, pot roast like Mom used to make, cobbler, and shakes.

Continental Store
5014 Roosevelt Way NE
Seattle
523-0606
Bratwurst, veal loaf, German beers, salads.

Ezell's Fried Chicken
4216 University Way NE
Seattle
548-1455
Chicken, potato salad, baked beans, mashed potatoes and gravy, sweet potato pie, pound cake.

Honey Bear Bakery
2106 North 55th Street
Seattle
545-7296
Breads, pies, muffins, torta rustica, soups, and salads.

Islabelle Caribbean
1501 North 45th Street
Seattle
632-8011
Red and black beans, watercress, foo foo balls, marinated meat and fish—all served with rice and Caribbean spices.

Julia's in Wallingford
1714 North 44th Street
Seattle
633-1175

Julia's Park Place
5410 Ballard Avenue NW
Seattle
783-2033
Wholesome nutburgers, pasta, fish 'n' chips, freshly prepared sandwiches and salads, vegetarian items.

Larry's Markets
10008 Aurora Avenue North
Seattle
527-5333
Gourmet meats and fish, stuffed and prepared for grilling. Large selection of imported ingredients, including Asian.

Macheesmo Mouse
4129 University Way NE
Seattle
286-6873
Everything is made to order with fresh ingredients and homemade salsa. Chicken and vegetarian burritos, enchiladas, soft tacos complete with beans and rice. Quesadillas, chicken fajitas, salads. All menu items can be taken out.

Mae's Phinney Ridge Cafe
6412 Phinney Avenue North
Seattle
782-1222
Call ahead for made-to-order picnic fare, including pot pies, fresh salmon patties, pan-fried catfish, fresh-roasted turkey sandwiches, potato salad, homemade pies, espresso shakes.

Musashi's Sushi and Grill
1400 North 45th Street
Seattle
633-0212
Japanese specialties to go, sushi.

Pasta & Company
2640 University Village
Seattle
523-8594
*Fresh pastas, sauces, soups,
salads. Many specialty items.*

Peerless Pie
4508 University Village
Seattle
523-7992
*Chicken pot pie, Tuscan taco pot
pie, different berry pies every week.*

Puget Consumer's Co-op
6504 20th Avenue NE
Seattle
525-1450
*Raw milk and cream, wide variety
of organically grown produce and
food products.*

QFC
4547 University Village
Seattle
523-5160
Deli items, beer, wine.

The Redhook Ale Brewery
and Trolleyman Pub
3400 Phinney Avenue North
Seattle
548-8000
*Daily hot and cold specials, pasta,
beef pies, desserts, bottled ale. (No
minors in alehouse.) No food
served on Sundays.*

The Souk
11730 Pinehurst Way NE
Seattle
367-8387
*Middle Eastern and African spices
and ingredients.*

Toshi's Teriyaki
10716 Fifth Avenue NE
Seattle
361-9134
*Take-out chicken and beef
teriyaki, coleslaw, and rice.*

Truffles
3701 NE 45th Street
Seattle
522-3016
*Sandwiches, salads, specialty
items, picnics to go.*

The Wedge
4760 University Village
Seattle
523-2560
*Gourmet sandwiches, salads,
desserts, pane riteano, calzone.*

Yak's Deli
3424 Fremont North
Seattle
632-0560
*Combination chicken and pork
barbecue, teriyaki, fried vegetables.*

SOUTH SEATTLE
Alki Bakery and Cafe
2726 Alki SW
Seattle
935-0616
*Cashew chicken crunch,
sandwiches, and generous salads.*

Beacon Market
2500 Beacon Avenue South
Seattle
323-2050
*Neighborhood market with fresh
fish, Southeast Asian ingredients,
and Chinese barbecue.*

B & O Espresso
2352 California SW
Seattle
935-1540
*Spicy chicken noodles, vegetable
sandwiches, chicken shwarma
sandwich, spinach boreks, baked
tortellini, soups.*

Gem Fish and Fresh Produce
6051 Martin Luther King Jr.
Way South
Seattle
725-1287
Family-owned Asian market.

Husky Deli
4721 California Avenue SW
Seattle
937-2810
*Sliced meats, salads, baked goods,
homemade ice cream.*

Mutual Fish Company
2335 Rainier Avenue South
Seattle
322-4368
*Great fish cakes and some of the
freshest fish in town. Sake kasu
available.*

Pambihira Oriental
Food Mart
6030 Martin Luther King Jr.
Way South
Seattle
722-2354
*Filipino and Asian specialty
items.*

Seattle Super Smoke
2554 Occidental South
Seattle
625-1339
*Smoked poultry, pork ribs,
sandwiches to order.*

EASTSIDE
Alpenland Delicatessen
2707 78th Avenue SE
Mercer Island
232-4780
*Bratwurst, veal loaf, potato salad,
famous mustard house dressing.*

Andre's Gourmet Cuisine
14125 NE 20th Street
Bellevue
747-6551
*French and Vietnamese specialties
to go, including spicy noodles with
chicken and prawns.*

British Pantry, Ltd.
8125 161st Avenue NE
Redmond
883-7511
*Lancashire pasties, sausage rolls,
cold pub pies.*

Caveman Kitchen
807 West Valley Highway
Kent
854-1210
*Chicken, ribs, potato salad, baked
beans, bootlegger pudding, and
apple melt to go.*

C'est Cheese
7525 SE 24th
Mercer Island
232-9810
*Chicken in an herbed bread
basket, bleu cheese potato salad,
homemade baguettes, all packed in
your basket or in their split wood
picnic baskets (on loan to you).
Bring in your baked-bean pot to
fill. (Owners think it looks better
than a foil pan.)*

Chateau Ste. Michelle
Gift Shop & Deli
14111 NE 145th
Woodinville
488-1133
Wine, pre-prepared picnic lunches packed in a chateau-shaped box, pâté, cheese, brownies, fruit, pasta salad.

DeLaurenti Italian &
International Food Market
317 Bellevue Way NE
Bellevue
454-7155
Cheeses, breads, specialty items. Imported ingredients.

Delicatessen of Europe
129 106th Avenue NE
Bellevue
455-9590
European, Jewish, and Russian cuisine. Piroshkis, blintzes, stuffed cabbage, eggplant, potato, cheese, and seafood salads.

Larry's Markets
699 120th Avenue NE
Bellevue
453-0600
Wonderful selection of gourmet foods and meals-to-go.

Overlake Blueberry Farm
2127 Bellevue Way SE
Bellevue
454-3539
U-pick blueberries by the pound in season, plus recipes.

Paul Thomas Wines
1717 136th Place NE
Bellevue
747-1008
Dry fruit wines, tours by appointment.

QFC
10116 NE Eighth
Bellevue
455-0870
Extensive deli choices.

Sweetwater Restaurant
7824 Leary Way
Redmond
883-9090
Entire menu can be ordered to go.
Menu changes daily.

Toshi's Teriyaki
10618 Main Street
Bellevue
453-8719
Take-out chicken and beef
teriyaki, coleslaw, and rice.

Uwajimaya
15555 NE 24th
(at Bellevue-Redmond Road)
Bellevue
747-9012
Sushi to go, Asian vegetables and
fruit, Kirin beer, sake.

INDEX

Alaska Northwest Books™ proudly recommends more of its outstanding books on Northwest living:

GOLF COURSES OF THE PACIFIC NORTHWEST, by Jeff Shelley

Here's the book hardcore golf enthusiasts rave about. You'll find vital statistics about hundreds of public, semiprivate, and private golf courses and driving ranges in Washington, Oregon, northern Idaho, the greater Sun Valley area, and northwestern Montana. Color photographs and 21 maps are included.

344 pages, softbound, $19.95 ($24.95 Canadian), ISBN 0-88240-401-6

THE GREAT NORTHWEST NATURE FACTBOOK: *Remarkable Animals, Plants, and Natural Features in Washington, Oregon, Idaho, and Montana,* by Ann Saling. Illustrations by Mark A. Zingarelli

Did you know that a geoduck can live to be 115 years old? Or that Montana has the record for the lowest temperature ever recorded in the Lower 48 (–70 degrees F. in 1954)? The Pacific Northwest is a land of rain forests and sand dunes, of lava beds and tide pools, inhabited by giant octopi, warted she-devils, banana slugs—even carnivorous plants. *The Great Northwest Nature Factbook* chronicles the weird and wonderful plants, animals, and physical features of this diverse region. Illustrated with 50 drawings.

200 pages, softbound, $9.95 ($12.95 Canadian), ISBN 0-88240-407-5

ARTISTS AT WORK: *25 Northwest Glassmakers, Ceramists and Jewelers,* by Susan Biskeborn. Photographic portraits by Kim Zumwalt

The Pacific Northwest is home to many of the country's best glassmakers, ceramists, and jewelers. Author Susan Biskeborn thoughtfully examines the lives and art of 25 of these nationally recognized artists. Kim Zumwalt's black-and-white photographic portraits capture the artists in their working environment. Color photographs feature each artist's work.

172 pages, softbound, $24.95 ($29.95 Canadian), ISBN 0-88240-405-9

Many other fascinating books are available from Alaska Northwest Books™. Ask at your favorite bookstore or write us for a free catalog.

Alaska Northwest Books™

A division of GTE Discovery Publications, Inc.
P.O. Box 3007
Bothell, Washington 98041-3007
Call toll free 1-800-331-3510